Lockheed 188

Electra

By David G. Powers

Great Airliners

S E R I E S

Volume Five

ABOUT THE AUTHOR

David Powers was born in Des Moines, Iowa, in 1960. His keen interest in aviation can be traced back to a steamer trunk his father brought home following a tour of duty as a U.S. Navy Seabee in the Philippines. In that trunk were flying model airplane components such as propellers, wings and wheels.

Growing up in Omaha, Nebraska, Dave's interest in all things aeronautical continued to grow. Upon graduation from the University of Nebraska at Lincoln with a degree in History, he was commissioned as Ensign in the U.S. Navy, attended flight training and was awarded the Wings of Gold in 1984. During both sea and shore tours, he flew rotary- and fixed-wing aircraft. In the early 1990s, Dave left the Navy to pursue a career in the airline business, landing a pilot's job at Pan American. With the demise of that company, he moved on to the more secure world of night cargo flying at Airborne Express.

Dave currently flies DC-9s, in addition to Bell AH-1F Cobras for an Army National Guard Air Cavalry unit. Having traveled the world, he now resides back in Omaha with his wife, Lorrie, and their two Scotties, Steed and Mrs. Peel.

© 1999 by David G. Powers
All rights reserved.
ISBN 1-892437-01-5
First Edition March 1999
Printed and bound in Hong Kong

All information contained in this volume is accurate at the time of publication.

Series Editor: Jon Proctor

Book and cover design by Randy Wilhelm, Left Field Productions, Sandpoint, Idaho
Copy Editors: Fred Chan and Billie Jean Plaster

Photo Credits
Front cover: . . . . .Henry Tenby
Title page: . . . . .Harry Sievers Collection
Back cover: Lockheed Martin Corporation *(top)*
. . . . :. Gianfranco Beting *(bottom)*
Inside back cover: . . . . .Gianfranco Beting

The Great Airliners series:

TABLE OF CONTENTS

APPENDICES

Lockheed Martin Corporation

ACKNOWLEDGMENTS

One of the most enjoyable aspects of writing this book was the wide variety of people I have had the pleasure to meet along the way. I have spoken with folks from around the globe, whether in person, on the telephone or through the mail, who are truly impassioned with the venerable Lockheed Electra. This incredibly large spectrum of individuals runs the gamut from former and current Lockheed and airline employees to pilots and the myriad of enthusiasts who also consider the 188 their favorite airliner. All have provided valuable input.

I would like to acknowledge several people without whose help this book would not have been possible and to whom I owe my sincerest gratitude. First of all, I thank editor Jon Proctor – an infinitely patient person – for his willingness to take a chance with this relatively unknown author while providing help and advice over the past several months. Also, my thanks to Nick Veronico at World Transport Press who helped me get this whole process started in the first place.

Although I worked with dozens of people at Lockheed Martin, some deserve special recognition. At Marietta, Georgia, there is Peter J. Clukey, a man who has the enviable task of being the Field Support Analyst for the Electra. The amount of information he provided is – without a doubt – the backbone of this book. There were occasions when I would call him several times a day to request additional data and he always came through. Out in the Lockheed Martin Skunk Works at Palmdale, California, Denny Lombard and his collection of vintage Electra photographs upgraded the book's visual selection from good to great.

I am in debt to Gainfranco Beting from Brazil. In addition to unlimited access to his extensive personal photo collection, he made several trips at his own expense in order to come up with shots I needed. Gianfranco's images are simply works of art. From down under, Peter J. Sweetten also allowed me generous access to his collection of Australian Electras.

I sincerely thank Robert J. Serling, the consummate aviation writer. I used several of Bob's volumes for my research and was able to tap his personal wealth of knowledge to enhance the book's accuracy.

The following individuals provided assistance and, in many cases, photographs: Keith Armes, Erik Bernhard, Henry Boyton, Kriss Bredehoft, Phil Brooks, Gary Buldoc, Bruce Drum, Todd Duhnke, Tony Eastwood, Joe Ferriera, Hill Goodspeed, Eddy Gual, Willis Hawkins, David Hofeling, Bill Hough, Don Linn, Jim Litz, Bryant Petitt, Jr., Capt. E. Earl Rodgers, Jack Real, Eric Schulzinger, Bob Shane, Harry Sievers, Bill Slaten, Myron J. Smith, Robert Taylor, Henry Tenby, Terry Waddington and Tom Verges, Sr.

The following companies and organizations provided generous assistance: Air Spray, Aireports, Antique Aircraft Association, Atlantic Airlines, Aviation Photography Worldwide, Candid Aero-Files, Cathay Pacific Airways, Channel Express, Conair Aviation, Ecuatoriana, Emil Buehler Naval Aviation Library, Federal Aviation Administration, Filair, Foundation Magazine, Lockheed Martin, Logbook Magazine, Lynden Air Cargo, Mandala Airlines, National Archives, National Aeronautics and Space Administration, National Center for Atmospheric Research, National Atmospheric and Oceanographic Administration, Reeve Aleutian Airways, United States Customs Service, United States Naval Institute, United States Navy, VARIG, and Zantop International Airlines.

I must plead to the standard author's alibi and say that if I missed thanking you, I apologize and genuinely appreciate your help.

Finally, I would like to thank my wife, Lorrie, who has been my greatest advocate throughout this project.

Dave Powers
Omaha, Nebraska

FOREWORD

The Model 188, otherwise known as the Lockheed Electra, is one of the most interesting – and controversial – transports in the history of commercial aviation.

Its story involves triumph and tragedy. When the last Electra is finally retired, its epitaph might read: This was an airplane loved by every pilot who ever flew it, and damned by a lot of other people.

Significantly, 188 flight crews and customers still consider it one of the most competent and underrated airliners ever conceived. At the same time, it also has been the butt of sick jokes, came perilously close to being grounded as unsafe, and was linked with the British Comet jetliner as symbols of disastrous engineering mistakes.

Airmen always praised its enormous power and maneuverability – an airliner that handled like a fighter. Yet there also was a time when you couldn't pay people to ride on an Electra; when passengers would change reservations if they learned they were ticketed on an Electra flight. And all those puzzling contradictions add up to the biography of an airplane that begs to be told.

Dave Powers has accomplished this feat, with thorough research and admirable skill. He is a rare find among aviation authors – not merely an objective writer but also an airline and Navy pilot qualified in both fixed-wing aircraft and helicopters.

His book brings back many personal memories. I covered the Braniff and Northwest crashes that touched off the heated Electra controversy when I was aviation editor of United Press International almost 40 years ago. I never imagined that four decades later this incredibly maligned transport would still be serving the industry faithfully and efficiently, which has to rank among the greatest of all aeronautical comebacks.

So read and enjoy this remarkable history of a legendary transport plane that overcame adversity, prejudice and even slander.

Robert J. Serling

Chapter I
THE EARLY YEARS

Model G – the first Lockheed – photographed in San Francisco Bay. (Lockheed Martin Corporation)

Allan Haines Loughead was born in 1889 in Niles, California, the youngest of four children. After the separation of his parents, he moved with his mother to Alma, California, in the Santa Cruz foothills. Growing up in a period of rapid technological advancement, young Allan's interest soon drifted from that of his mother's fruit farm to automobiles. By age 15 he had built his first racing car. Like his older brother Malcolm, Allan left the farm and went to nearby San Francisco where he found work repairing automobiles. Being a mechanically minded person, he also began to study airplanes, and it was through his oldest brother, Victor, that Allan would be exposed to the world of aviation.

Victor Loughead worked in Chicago, Illinois, as an engineer and developed a keen interest in the new technology of flight. He wrote two books, *Vehicles of the Air* (1909) and *Airplane Designing for Amateurs* (1910), both best sellers that were veritable how-to guides for fledgling aviators and designers. After reading these books, Allan decided to seek out his brother and look more deeply in the new world of flight. Racing his car at various meets across the country, Allan worked his way to Chicago where, with his brother's help, he found a job as an airplane engine mechanic. It was during this time that Allan took his first flight.

Allan Loughead points out features of the Model G. (Lockheed Martin Corporation)

Although many of the details have been lost to time, it seems that he rode in an airplane built from scratch and was required by the design of the craft to operate the aileron controls. Allan worked for James E. Plew, who

Early Lockheed greats including Jack Northrop, pointing at plans.
(Lockheed Martin Corporation)

just happened to own a Curtiss-type pusher biplane. One snowy day in December 1910, several pilots attempted to fly Plew's airplane but all failed to leave the ground. Plew was ready to call it a day when his mechanic, Allan Loughead persuaded his boss to let him have a try. After a couple of aborted attempts, Loughead made a quick adjustment to the carburetor and coaxed the flimsy bi-plane into the air. He circled the field and came in for a landing. In a single flight Loughead had taught himself how to fly and completed his first solo flight.

In this early stage of aviation, a person who had actually flown an airplane was considered "experienced." With but a handful of hours in the air, Allan Loughead billed himself as a flight instructor and an exposition pilot. It was during an exposition flight in September 1911 that he crashed another under-powered and rickety Curtiss-type biplane. The novice pilot emerged unhurt from the accident but with an idea to build a better airplane. In 1911 Loughead and his wife moved back to California.

Working again as an auto mechanic, Allan teamed up with his other brother, Malcolm. With a $4,000 stake obtained mostly from the Alco Cab Company, the two formed the Alco Hydro-Aeroplane Company. Working in their spare time they built their first airplane, a single engine bi-plane mounted on floats called the Model G. The "G" designation was chosen to imply that the company had actually built previous models. On June 15, 1913, Allan took the Model G aloft for the first time. The short test flight was a success, after which he carried Malcolm for an aerial tour of San Francisco Bay. Despite a successful first project, both Allan and Malcolm eventually went back to their day jobs and the sole Model G was put into storage.

The subsequent years found Allan Loughead doggedly pursuing his aviation dream. It was a time of boom and bust; several qualified successes were produced under various corporate names and with diverse financial backing. Although Malcolm left to seek different fortunes, Allan moved ahead, hiring a young engineer by the name of John K. "Jack" Northrop away from the Douglas Company. Northrop would prove to be an aviation trailblazer in his own right. In December 1926 Allan opened the Lockheed Aircraft Company and went on to build a line of aircraft that set a standard for the industry.

The true pronunciation of the Scottish Loughead is "Lockheed," a spelling Allan decided to adopt after reportedly tiring of being addressed as "Log Head." Victor Lockheed had been using the Lockheed name since 1909 when he published his first book on aviation.

Beginning with the Vega, Lockheed built the Orion, Air Express, Explorer, Altair and the Sirius. These high-speed airplanes, all based on the same molded wooden fuselage, would be used as airliners, research craft, world record-setters and as corporate aircraft. Flown by such famous aviators as Wiley Post, Charles Lindbergh, Amelia Earhart and Roscoe Turner, the Lockheed Company of the late 1920s and early 1930s and its stable of airplanes began piling success upon success.

The First Electra

Despite riding this wave of accomplishment the Lockheed Company was hit hard by the Great Depression. After entering bankruptcy, it was bought in June 1932 by a group of aviation businessmen headed by Robert

The original Electra – Lockheed's Model 10. (Lockheed Martin Corporation)

The Vickers Viscount 700, wearing Trans-Canada colors. (Jon Proctor Collection)

enough for airline use. The idea of jet propulsion both thrilled and terrified airline executives. On one hand, jets offered the kind of range, speed and payload potential only dreamed of with reciprocating engines. On the other hand, the cost of airliner fleets based on a new and seemingly mysterious technology gave top executives reason to pause. Their anxiety was born from the jet's need for large amounts of fuel plus longer runways and updated airport facilities.

Another problem that was to plague this transition was the enormous amount of noise produced by the early turbine engines. Also, these new craft would be flying in an Air Traffic Control system that could only barely handle the speed of piston airliners. Enter into this era the idea of the "turbo-propeller" power plant. Although not as fast as a pure jet, the "turboprop" would allow airlines to ease into the jet age rather than jump in unprepared. Also, many airlines did not require the performance capabilities of a pure jet. Some route structures, stage lengths and passenger numbers simply could not take advantage of early pure-jet performance.

Like it or not, the decade of the 1950s brought turbine-powered airliners to the industry. Whether to buy them was not the question, but rather, which one? On the drawing board in the United States were the Boeing 707 and the Douglas DC-8, two large, long-range jets, along with the mid-range Convair 880. From Great Britain and already flying were the de Havilland Comet – in service with British Overseas Airways Corporation (BOAC) since 1952 – and the turboprop Vickers Viscount that joined British European Airways (BEA) in 1953. Although several carriers had ordered limited numbers of turbine-powered aircraft, Capital became the first U.S. airline to make a serious commitment to turbine technology.

The Capital route structure was characterized by short hops over congested, highly competitive routes. It was obvious that the 707, DC-8 and Comet were all too big and thirsty to be economically sound for short-haul flying. Capital executives approached Lockheed to see if that company could build an airliner similar to the Vickers Viscount. More

E. Gross. At this point Allan Lockheed left the company. He would later establish other aviation-manufacturing firms but, unfortunately, never enjoyed such great success again.

Meanwhile, Gross and his team began a search for a new aircraft to bring the company out of its slump. One candidate was a "metal Orion" airliner that was subsequently rejected by Gross in light of current aviation developments. Sleek, all-metal airliners powered by multiple engines were already on other manufacturer's drawing boards or in their factories. Considering recent U.S. government restrictions on single-engine transports, plus the fact that the Douglas DC-2 and Boeing 247 were both in development, the metal Orion was obsolete while still only on paper.

Lockheed eventually settled on the Model 10, a twin-engine, low-wing monoplane configuration, designed by a team headed by Hall L. Hibbard. It was christened "Electra," and a model was sent to the University of Michigan wind tunnel for tests. It was here that a young engineer named Clarence "Kelly" Johnson began his long and fruitful career with Lockheed. Johnson determined that a single vertical tail design would not provide sufficient stability and suggested a feature synonymous with many Lockheeds to come, multiple vertical stabilizers and rudders. The Electra's first flight occurred on February 23, 1934. It became the fastest airliner in the sky, even outpacing the competing Douglas DC-2, albeit smaller and with fewer passenger seats. Airlines including Pan American, Northwest, Braniff and Delta operated the Electra along with military branches, both foreign and domestic. Further development of the line resulted in the Model 12 "Electra Junior," Model 14 "Super Electra" and Model 18 Lodestar. Although fast, safe, tolerably comfortable and productive, the early Electra series, along with all the other airliners in the field, was eventually eclipsed by the Douglas DC-3.

Into the Jet Age

The years between the production of the first-generation Electra of the 1930s and introduction of the Model 188 Electra in the mid-1950s saw the introduction of turbine power plants. This one innovation – in some ways greater than any other – changed the face of both civil and military aviation. Although tinkered with on a limited scale well before World War II, it was not until after the conflict that turbine engines were made reliable and efficient

Early artist rendition of the American Airlines original concept. (Lockheed Martin Corporation)

than any other American company, Lockheed was gaining valuable experience in the area of turboprop power, having developed the military C-130 Hercules and the R7V-2/YC-121F. But with only one customer, Lockheed was forced to abandon the idea of developing a completely new airliner. Throughout the early to mid-1950s, the manufacturer was committed to its development of the Constellation series, culminating with the Model 1649A Starliner. The 1649B model, a long-range turboprop, was not built because of little customer interest due to the introduction of long-range jets.

Thus, in May 1954, Capital Airlines placed the first order for what would eventually grow to 60 Viscounts. The type began revenue service on July 26, 1955. With its greater speed and smoother, quieter ride, the turbopropliner was an instant success and validated itself with lower than predicted operating costs and highly reliable Rolls-Royce Dart engines.

The "Prop-Jet" Electra

With Capital starting to reap the rewards of turbine power, the "Big Four" domestic U.S. airlines (Eastern, TWA, United and American) were not content to sit idly by and simply watch the experiment. At the time nearly 75 percent of airline segments were considered short-to-medium range. To this end, American Airlines envisioned a stretched Convair 240 design powered by four turbine engines. American approached Lockheed, Boeing, Douglas and Convair in late 1954 for the purpose of filling this demand. Boeing was already fully occupied with the 707, and Convair dropped out early, considering the project to be prohibitively expensive. Douglas engineers put forward an idea based on mounting turboprop engines on its DC-7, but the design, called the DC-7D, was rejected.

Lockheed's proposal – the CL-303 – was a high-wing, two- or four-engine turboprop airliner seating 60 to 70 passengers. Powered by either Napier Elands or Rolls-Royce Darts, it would have a speed of 350 mph over an 800-mile range. Although the design met American's basic requirement, it was turned down and Lockheed shelved the proposal.

American Airlines again approached the major manufacturers in 1955 with a different request for a larger, four-engine airliner seating 75 passengers with a range of around 2,000 miles. Again, power was to be provided by either the Eland or the Dart. Eastern Air Lines then entered the picture but wanted still more capacity with increased speed and range. Although both Boeing and Douglas submitted designs, American and Eastern chose the CL-310 design concept from Lockheed; it would later be designated the Model 188 Electra. American placed an initial order for 35 on June 8, 1955. Eastern followed suit on September 27, signing up for 40 with deliveries scheduled to begin in late 1958. With orders for 75 airliners from only two airlines, Lockheed enthusiastically went forward with the project.

In its final form, the Model 188 Electra emerged as a four-engine, short-to-medium range, pressurized airliner seating 85 to 90 passengers. The fuselage cross-section would be a constant 128 inches in diameter, equal to the mid-section of the Constellation fuselage. Lockheed believed this to be ideal as it provided maximum seating while minimizing the challenge of designing a pressurized fuselage. It also allowed for five-abreast seating in the basic configuration, four-abreast in a luxury form, or even six-abreast in what Lockheed called "Thrift Class." Studies showed that the Electra could turn a profit when filling only 50 percent of its maximum capacity. In order to achieve Eastern's requirement for greater speed, the Allison 501D turboprop was selected. This civilian version of the military

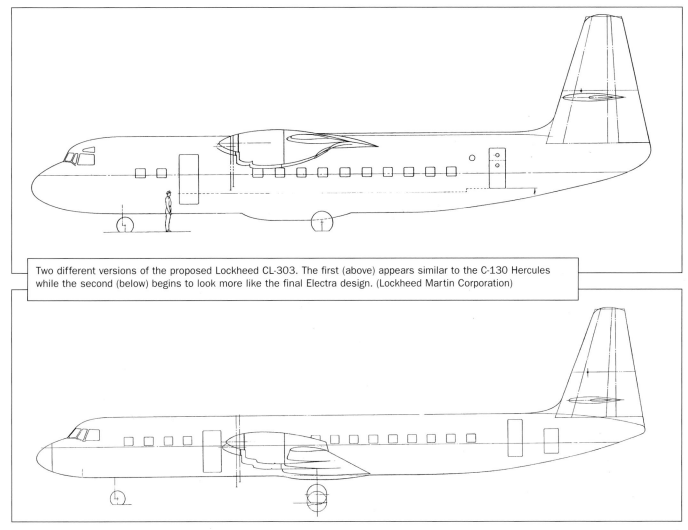

Two different versions of the proposed Lockheed CL-303. The first (above) appears similar to the C-130 Hercules while the second (below) begins to look more like the final Electra design. (Lockheed Martin Corporation)

Closer to the final design, this model exhibits a squared vertical tail that, in the end, was not incorporated. (Lockheed Martin Corporation)

Eastern Air Lines President Eddie Rickenbacker examines an Electra model complete with ground service equipment. (Lockheed Martin Corporation)

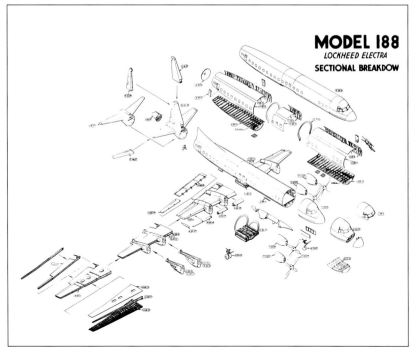

MODEL 188
LOCKHEED ELECTRA
SECTIONAL BREAKDOW

T56 engine would give the Electra a top speed of 440 miles per hour. The T56 was already logging flight time on the C-130. Depending on payload, the range would be more than 2,700 miles.

Lockheed offered several versions of the Electra. The Model 188A was the basic type while the Model 188C was a long-range variant with greater fuel capacity and a higher gross weight. The 188B designation was actually an internal company designation used to describe certain Model 188C aircraft destined for overseas operators. It featured track-mounted seats, a navigator station and additional lavatories. An executive Electra was also offered but attracted no buyers. As with most civilian airliners, the military was courted with variants proposed as transports, airborne ambulances and training aircraft. The ultimate winner for Lockheed and the United States Navy was, of course, the P-3 Orion.

For both American and Eastern, a delivery price of just over $2 million per Electra was promised, excluding customer-furnished equipment. Lockheed predicted that sales of 190 airliners would be required before the company would start making a profit on the project.

Designing the Electra

No radical construction theories were put forth to make an airliner with the performance capabilities of the Electra. However, Lockheed engineers from the start designed it to be easy and cost-effective to produce. Although physical construction was based on many proven concepts and techniques, several innovative ideas were incorporated to speed assembly and increase production efficiency. The fuselage was built in several large, individual panels rather than in "barrel" sections, with the completed panels then joined together to form the fuselage. This allowed construction in a relatively small area and made it easier to move finished sections around prior to assembly completion. The production line was based on a series of ground-based jigs rather than overhead cranes, allowing use of existing buildings with low ceilings.

Prior to riveting fuselage skin to the frame members, a compound was applied to the metal sheets. This proven technique made for more complete sealing of the cabin and also shortened the overall assembly time. Inside the cabin, conditioned air was distributed by conventional ducting, but cabin heat was provided by resistance wire embedded in radiant panels placed between the fuselage skin and cabin interior panels. The radiant panels themselves were built on a special fixture designed to quickly and precisely imbed the wire-heating elements. Plastics were also used extensively in the Electra, in nearly triple the amount found in the Model 1649A Starliner. This not only saved a considerable amount of weight but also made odd-shaped components fast and easy to produce.

Of course, all this production efficiency would not mean a thing if the product did not perform as advertised. When it came to pre-production trials and evaluation, Lockheed claimed that the Electra was its most thoroughly tested airplane. Company engineers set up a program to validate all the aspects that combined to make the airplane, ranging from the drafting table to the wind tunnel and to the factory floor.

For the first time, Lockheed fabricated a full-scale, non-flying fuselage to explore aspects of the Electra's "fail-safe" design. Referred to as "Serial No. 9999," it was complete from forward to rear pressure bulkheads. Engineers simulated turbulent flight conditions by using hydraulic jacks to impart a twisting movement to the pressurized mockup. In this state, 9999 was subjected to tests ranging from a simple cut around a window or door frame to firing a spear through the skin. In all, 19 saw cuts and 19 spear shots were made; in each case the damage was contained by the fail-safe design.

A wing mockup and a tail assembly were also subjected to fail-safe tests. Each major assembly was repeatedly tortured well beyond its design limits, until it finally failed. The results of these trials – combined with thousands of hours of wind tunnel testing on models – suggested several modifications while validating the basic engineering design.

An acoustic mockup was designed to determine cabin noise levels, using a sound source simulating the engines and airflow over the fuselage. Inside this mockup the test variables ran from bare metal skin to full interior trim, telling Lockheed engineers the extent of insulation required to make the Electra comfortable for the flying public. It also showed that the radiant heating panels actually acted like a double-wall structure and helped dampen out noise and vibration. In addition, this mockup was used to determine cabin noise levels caused by several components such as hydraulic pumps and electric motors. The results of these evaluations prompted the development of pump enclosures, vibration mounts and acoustic filters.

A 40-foot-long thermal mockup was built to test the efficiency of the air conditioning system and the radiant heating panels. Additionally, dozens of sub-systems were verified in mockups, including landing gear and nose wheel steering, airfoil anti-icing systems, plus hydraulic and electrical systems.

As a matter of course, most basic airliner designs are built to specifications issued by one or more airlines. The Electra evolved from two carriers: American and Eastern. When it came to specific aspects of the Electra's final form, however, Lockheed enlisted the aid of those who would work with the new airliner, including pilots, mechanics and ramp workers. Pilots from several airlines were invited to examine their "office," the cockpit. They suggested several changes, which ran from basic layout to the position of instruments, switches and handles. Many were incorporated in the final design.

Pilots were also introduced to the latest theories in automatic systems, including pressurization, heating and cooling, and airframe anti-icing. This new "human engineering" also extended to emergency procedures such as fighting an engine fire. In earlier airliners, dealing with an engine fire meant moving several different levers to secure the ignition system, fuel flow and hydraulics while actuating the extinguisher bottles. In the Electra all could be accomplished with just one lever. The outcome of this exchange was a cockpit designed for airline pilots.

From the maintenance group came veteran mechanics with years of experience working on airliners that were not necessarily designed with them in mind. For these professionals, Lockheed had

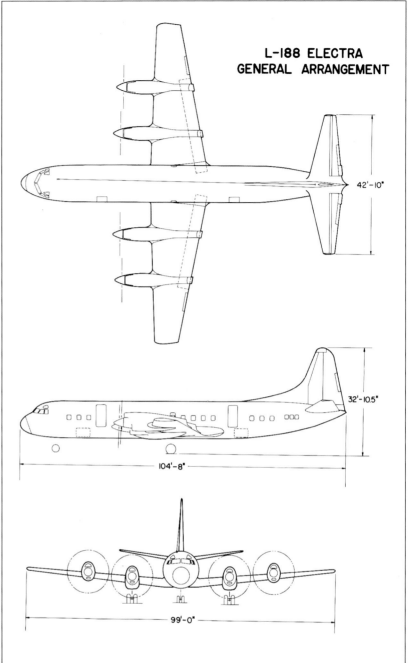

L-188 ELECTRA
GENERAL ARRANGEMENT

42'-10"

32'-10.5"

104'-8"

99'-0"

The mockups and first 188 fuselages were built alongside Constellations, using these docks. (Lockheed Martin Corporation)

Mockup fuselages under construction. (Lockheed Martin Corporation)

developed the "service center concept." This design basically grouped components of like systems such as hydraulics, electrical and air conditioning into individual service centers that could be accessed externally. The mechanic could get to a centralized set of components without entering the aircraft, removing seats and panels and without offloading passengers or cargo. The airframe's close proximity to the ground meant routine work could be accomplished without a work stand. When it came to something as simple as nuts and bolts, Lockheed had a better idea. Rather than labor-intensive cotter keys and safety wire, self-locking nuts and threaded inserts were incorporated to speed up maintenance. Even complete engine changes could be accomplished in about two hours because the entire engine/nacelle assembly was designed to be removed and replaced as a single unit called a "Power Egg."

Considering fast turnarounds in the original design, engineers established the idea of "self-containment." The Electra was going to be used on short-to-medium legs with multiple stops. To support this scenario a single ground cart of existing design would power the heating system, Freon air conditioner, hydraulic and electrical systems and the folding stairway. Alternatively, a single engine could be kept turning to power the entire aircraft. As with the service center concept, hatches located close to the ground would provide easy access to the cargo compartments. Water and lavatory service were likewise designed to use existing ramp equipment. Refueling at a rate of more than 300 gallons per minute could be accomplished by means of a single-point fitting. Finally, all turnaround servicing could be done from the right side of the Electra, allowing unhampered passenger traffic on the left.

Building the Electra

Metal was cut for the first 188 in October 1955 at Lockheed's California Division in Burbank. The planned rollout date was December 11, 1957, with its maiden flight scheduled for January 31, 1958. The first four Electras, manufacturer's serial numbers (msns) 1001–1004 were to be used in the test, evaluation and certification phase, slated for completion by September 1958. Delivery of production models was to begin shortly thereafter. The sixth Electra (msn 1006) would go to the Allison Division of General Motors for further research and testing of the 501D turboprop

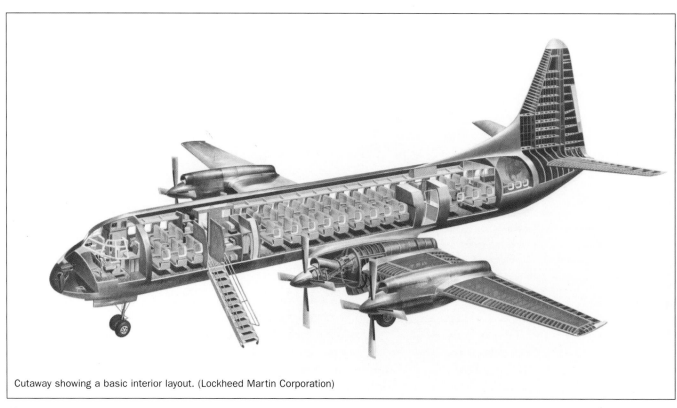

Cutaway showing a basic interior layout. (Lockheed Martin Corporation)

A Lockheed engineer inspects the large scale Electra model during wind tunnel testing. (Lockheed Martin Corporation)

engine. The fifth Electra (msn 1005), reserved for Eastern, was to be the first production airliner, although regular airline deliveries actually began with the seventh airframe.

Construction of the first prototype progressed so smoothly that it was rolled out into the Californian sunshine on November 11, 1957, one month ahead of schedule. On December 6, Lockheed's Model 188A Electra lifted off the runway at Burbank, California, taking to the air a full seven weeks earlier than planned. For those reporters, photographers, Lockheed employees and

Illustration showing ground service unit locations which allow uninterrupted passenger access. Note the upward opening passenger door design, later abandoned. (Lockheed Martin Corporation)

other interested parties, the Electra did not just take off; rather the new airliner leapt into the air, and was overhead by the time it reached mid-field. For this flight, the airplane weighed in at 90,000 pounds and used

The first prototype fuselage barrel being lifted from the construction dock. (Lockheed Martin Corporation)

less than 1,900 feet on its takeoff roll. Lockheed Chief Engineering Test Pilot Herman "Fish" Salmon was at the controls, assisted by co-pilot Roy Wimmer and engineers W. E. Sprener and I. W. Holland. The flight lasted 1 hour and 15 minutes, ending at Palmdale, California. In the December 30, 1957, issue of *Aviation Week* an editorial applauded the achievements of Lockheed's people, recognizing them for getting the Electra into the air ahead of schedule.

An early American Airlines interior mockup. (Lockheed Martin Corporation)

The 188 cockpit is so wide that two sets of throttle levers are required. (Todd Duhnke Collection)

Serial Number 9999 being slowly destroyed to test fail-safe construction techniques. (Lockheed Martin Corporation)

The Allison 501 "Power Egg." (Lockheed Martin Corporation)

Ship Number One – msn 1001 – out of the dock and awaiting engine installation. (Lockheed Martin Corporation)

15

THE ALLISON 501 ENGINE

The General Motors-Allison Electra, msn 1006. (Lockheed Martin Corporation)

The T56 flew for the first time in 1954, mounted in the nose of a B-17. Two converted United States Air Force (USAF) T56 -powered YC-131C transports logged more than 3,000 flight hours between May and December of 1955. By the following October, the T56 had chalked up 45,000 test stand hours and had actually flown in excess of 16,000 hours. The evolution of the T56 in to the 501 was a relatively simple process; more than 75 percent of the components were interchangeable. The most noticeable difference between the two power plants was the location of the reduction gearbox and the air intake. On the T56 the reduction gearbox was above the centerline of the engine with the air intake below the propeller; on the 501 this arrangement was reversed. Placing the intake high above the ground helped reduce ingestion of foreign objects. One other difference was the fact that on the 501 the idle revolutions per minute (RPM) was reduced in order to cut ramp noise levels. The Allison 501 became the first U.S.-built turbo-propeller engine

The Electra was first powered by four axial-flow Allison 501-D13s, each producing 3,750 eshp (equivalent shaft horsepower). Later Electras were equipped with the -D15 version of the 501, which raised the output to 4,050 eshp. The engine drove either the Aeroproducts 606 Turbo-Propeller (square cut blade tips) or the Hamilton Standard Hydromatic Propeller (round blade tips) both of which were 13 feet, 6 inches in diameter, full-feathering and reversible. For safety the engine/prop combination was equipped with a Negative Torque System to provide auto-feathering capability in the event of an engine failure. Installation of the 501 on the Electra used a concept called the Quick Engine Change (QEC), also known as the "Power Egg." This meant that the engine, reduction gearbox, propeller and many of the ancillary systems could be removed and replaced as a single unit, cutting the time for an engine change down to two hours.

The Allison 501 power plant was not a new concept, being the civilian version of the Allison T56 turboprop that was powering the Lockheed C-130A Hercules. Developed from the Allison T38,

A Convair 240 powered by Allison 501-A4 engines first flew in 1950. (Jon Proctor Collection)

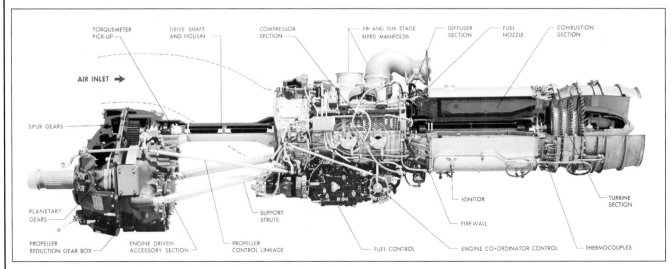

A cutaway of the Allison 501 power plant. (Lockheed Martin Corporation)

The Allison 501-powered "Elation." (Lockheed Martin Corporation)

An Allison 501 being run up on the Connie's Number Four position. (Lockheed Martin Corporation)

to be approved for civilian commercial operations when it was awarded Type Certificate No. 282 on May 20, 1955.

Despite its military lineage, the Allison 501 testing was just as comprehensive as that of the Electra itself. As early as 1950, Allison was hanging turboprop engines on airliners. In a joint effort with Convair, two Allison 501-A4s (the civil version of the T38) were installed on a Convair 240-21 airliner. Although under-powered, this conversion flew for the first time on December 29, 1950, and proved basically successful, giving Allison valuable data on turboprop airliner operations. When it came to the 501-D13 power plant, Allison again turned to a Convair

product. This time a C-131C (the military Convair 340) was borrowed from the USAF and equipped with two 501-D13 engines. Allison began "Operation Hourglass" on November 1, 1957, and completed more than 1,000 hours of airline-type flying by January 23, 1958. Although the 501 had already been certified, this operation proved its reliability under the rigors of airline operations and eventually led to the development of the successful Convair 580 airliner.

In 1957 Lockheed also conducted operational tests on the Allison 501 engine when it leased an R7V-2 (Lockheed Model 1249-95) from the United States Navy. This military version of the Lockheed Model 1049B Super Constellation had its radial reciprocating engines replaced with four 501s and, under the nickname "Elation" (Electra plus Constellation), flew some 3,300 flight test hours. The aircraft was eventually re-engined with Pratt & Whitney T34 turboprops and delivered to the USAF as a YC-121F.

Lockheed also took the prototype Model 1049 (originally a C-69 that was stretched) and pressed it in to service with an Allison 501 in the Number Four engine position. These two aircraft were flown in conditions ranging from normal airline operations to extreme weather and emergency conditions.

In all, the Allison 501s completed 80,000 hours of test stand time, 75,000 hours of service flight test time and an additional 50,000 hours of various individual engine component testing. Throughout this evaluation period, the Allison 501 turboprop engine proved itself as both powerful and reliable.

Had it not been for oncoming jets, the turbine-powered Connie could have been a long-range contender. (Lockheed Martin Corporation)

The complete Lockheed 188 Electra. (Lockheed Martin Corporation)

Lockheed Air Terminal, Burbank, circa 1960. Note the Electra ramp to the right of Runway 25. (Lockheed Martin Corporation)

First Flight of the Lockheed Electra. (Lockheed Martin Corporation)

Two legendary Lockheed test pilots: Tony LeVier (left) and Herman "Fish" Salmon. (Lockheed Martin Corporation)

Flight Test and Certification

By mid-1958 the first four 188s, all Lockheed owned, were working to prove what the engineers had predicted. The first, second and fourth aircraft were used for the certification program while the third served as a static test airframe; it would not fly until later in the year. In flight test, observers were particularly impressed by the Electra's copious amount of reserve power, aptly demonstrated by its ability to maintain altitude on only one engine. For the pilots who would fly it, this surplus of power was like a gift from Lockheed. At first sight of the airplane, one could be taken aback by what appeared to be a rather short wing, only 99 feet in span. Telling the pilot that a full 54 feet of the wing – nearly two-thirds of the span – was swept by the huge propellers (thus creating its own lift) would ease the apprehension somewhat. Also, the smooth, sleek nacelle of the Allison 501 replaced the drag-producing cowling of the radial piston engine of earlier airliners. Trepidation was quickly forgotten when a pilot flew through a rejected landing. Power response was instantaneous and a "go-around" could be easily executed from only inches above the runway. The Electra was soon being called a "fifty-ton fighter."

The Civil Aviation Authority awarded the Electra its Type Certificate on August 22, 1958. The first production model delivered to Eastern Air Lines was msn 1007, on October 8, 1958; msn 1005 was not handed over until early 1959. Meanwhile, Lockheed initiated an around-the-world flight using the fourth prototype. This sales tool was meant to demonstrate the airplane's performance and reliability. Considering the range of weather, airport facilities and countries visited it is admirable that the Electra completed the trip with no major problems.

The fourth prototype at Geneva during the European sales tour. (David Anderton; Tadd Kotick Collection)

The South American sales team. (Lockheed Martin Corporation)

Forward fuselage of msn 1004 showing logos of Electra purchasers. (David Anderton; Tadd Kotick Collection)

Prior to delivery to National Airlines, msn 1079 was used on a South American sales tour. (Lockheed Martin Corporation)

A celebration cake for the
Electra's CAA approval.
(Lockheed Martin Corporation)

Electra prototypes Number One (below) and Number Two. (Lockheed Martin Corporation)

For an airline to introduce a new airliner to revenue service is not only a public relations triumph but usually economically beneficial as well, being the leader with newer, more productive equipment. Several airlines can rightfully claim Electra firsts.

Although the claim is tenuous at best, Capital Airlines can be said to have started the Electra program when it approached Lockheed in 1953 with an unsuccessful idea for a turboprop airliner. Next came American Airlines, in 1954, but without success. However, American returned in 1955 to work with Lockheed and develop the concept that would ultimately become the Electra. Yet National Airlines actually placed the first 188 order when company officials signed a contract on December 9, 1955.

Finally, Eastern Air Lines can claim two Electra events, the first production aircraft delivery, on October 8, 1958, and the first revenue flight, on January 12, 1959, beating American by only a matter of days.

Original Operators

The following section is organized in alphabetical order and not by any criteria such as the largest fleet or the precedence of orders.

LOCKHEED 188 ELECTRA FIRST FLIGHTS		
(number per year)		
Year	*188A*	*188C*
1957	1	
1958	22	
1959	72	32
1960	16	16
1961	4	7

N6111A, American's *Flagship Tulsa,* made a pre-delivery appearance at a Las Vegas air show in April 1959, in conjunction with the World Congress of Flight convention. (Robert D. Archer)

American Airlines

In as early as 1952 American was planning the airline's entry into the jet age, although its managers were primarily examining pure-jet airliners with transcontinental range. In addition to long-range jets, C. R. Smith (American's president since 1934) wanted a turboprop aircraft to replace his company's Convair 240 and Douglas DC-6 fleets.

Smith's interest prompted a personal visit to the Vickers plant in England where he examined the new Viscount first hand. Accompanying Smith was Frank Kolk, an engineer working in the equipment planning office. Kolk advised his boss that although the Rolls-Royce Dart engines were acceptable, the airframe construction was not up to par when compared with U.S. industry standards. Having rejected the Viscount, Smith sent his teams to work on specifications that would meet American's criteria. These numbers were sent to Boeing, Douglas, Lockheed and Convair. Lockheed embraced the offer that would result in the Model 188 Electra.

With an airliner basically "built to order," it was only natural that American would buy it in large numbers. A letter of intent for 35 Electras came on June 8, 1955, and the contract was signed on December 15, 1955. The order was the second in size only to co-launch customer Eastern Air Lines. C. R. Smith believed that American could use 25 additional Electras in the future but a follow-up buy never materialized. This was initially due to uncertainty concerning its order for pure-jet Boeing 707s in November 1955, and later because the airline had started to purchase Boeing 727s. Although American had expected the Electra to become prominent player in its fleet, the turboprop was quickly eclipsed by the 707s, then 720s and 727s.

American's first Electra (msn 1015) was delivered on November 27, 1958 – registered N6101A – and christened *Flagship New York.* The carrier's public relations people balked at giving the Electra the *Flagship* title, which they thought was outdated and did not do justice to the new,

Flagship Tulsa thrills the air show audience with a single-engine flyby. Lockheed test pilots Tony LeVier and Fish Salmon were at the controls. (Robert D. Archer)

turbine technology. But history has since shown that this designation would endure past the Model 188. It was also during the time of the Electra introduction that American again considered painting its airliners. Although tests were earlier completed on a DC-6, C. R. Smith himself vetoed the idea. He believed that a bare metal aircraft would stand out from the pack, regardless of any maintenance benefits or unique liveries.

The airline was poised to start 188 service during the busy Christmas 1958 season but was thwarted by a pilot strike that began on December 19. One of the primary issues brought to the table was a result of new turbine aircraft – both the Electra and the 707. The pilots believed that with the new realm of jet airliners the flight engineer, who had always been mechanic-trained, should be replaced by a qualified pilot. The long and at times bitter dispute – which could be the subject of a book in itself – was settled 22 days later and scheduled Electra service finally began over the New York–Chicago route on January 23, 1959.

Unfortunately for the Electra, its debut was overshadowed by American's first transcontinental 707 flight two days later. Although outdone by its bigger stable mate, the Electra quickly proved to be a popular addition to the fleet. Pilots loved it and the flying public welcomed the 68-seat, all-first-class (and aft cocktail lounge)

On final, N6132A, *Flagship Richmond*, with Electra II titles. It was sold to McCulloch Properties in 1969. (Mel Lawrence; Bryant Petitt, Jr. Collection)

configuration. In mid-1961, the fleet would be reconfigured to accommodate 54 first-class and 17 coach passengers.

By March 1960 American had taken delivery of the last of its 35 Electras. The type served short- and medium-range segments in the eastern United States and the Midwest, not normally venturing west of El Paso. The Electras also provided an initial competitive advantage over American's arch-rivals TWA and United at New York's LaGuardia Airport, where jets were not allowed until airport modernization was completed in 1964. TWA lacked turboprops, as did United until its acquisition of Capital Airlines in mid-1961. Electras were also heavily scheduled into Chicago-Midway Airport and Washington's National Airport, which could not handle big jets.

Despite its popularity and efficiency, American began to reduce Electra flying starting in March 1962. At the time, the airline was experiencing a problem of over-capacity. Also – and most crucial to the Electra – was the anticipated appearance of the short-to-medium-range, pure-jet airliner. In American's case it was the Boeing 727; an order for 25 came on August 10, 1961. After the initial sale of a handful of Electras, the fleet remained relatively stable for the next several years, even with the introduction of BAC 1-11 service in 1966.

By 1968 the sell off began in earnest and the last of American's original Electra inventory was disposed of by January 1971.

| | | | AMERICAN AIRLINES | | |
| | | | (All built as 188As) | | |
msn	Registration	Flagship name	msn	Registration	Flagship name
1015	N6101A	*New York*	1073	N6119A	*Cleveland*
1019	N6102A	*Chicago*	1081	N6120A	*Newark*
1024	N6103A	*Detroit*	1083	N6121A	*Providence*
1025	N6104A	*Washington*	1093	N6122A	*Albany*
1027	N6105A	*Boston*	1100	N6123A	*Nashville*
1028	N6106A	*Dallas*	1102	N6124A	*El Paso*
1031	N6107A	*Fort Worth*	1115	N6125A	*Oklahoma City*
1037	N6108A	*Buffalo*	1116	N6126A	*Tucson*
1041	N6109A	*Toronto*	1117	N6127A	*Phoenix*
1049	N6110A	*St. Louis*	1119	N6128A	*San Diego*
1050	N6111A	*Tulsa*	1120	N6129A	*Los Angeles*
1051	N6112A	*Philadelphia*	1121	N6130A	*San Francisco*
1054	N6113A	*Syracuse*	1122	N6131A	*Little Rock*
1056	N6114A	*Rochester*	1123	N6132A	*Richmond*
1058	N6115A	*New York*	1124	N6133A	*Baltimore*
1063	N6116A	*Cincinnati*	1125	N6134A	*Memphis*
1065	N6117A	*Louisville*	1126	N6135A	San Antonio
1072	N6118A	*Hartford*	1006	N1432	untitled*

*This Model 188A was originally delivered to General Motors as an engine test bed and registered N5501V. Never placed in revenue service by American, it was accepted in partial trade for a Boeing 720 and later sold.

Originally *Flagship Newark*, N6120A (msn 1081) wears the later circle-logo or "lightning bolt" livery. (Jon Proctor Collection)

VH-RMA in Ansett's first Electra colors. (Lockheed Martin Corporation)

Ansett–ANA

The third largest domestic Australian carrier behind Trans-Australia Airlines (TAA) and Australian National Airways (ANA), Ansett was operating a fleet of Douglas DC-3s and Convair 440s when it began looking at the Electra in 1956. Its original four-aircraft purchase announcement for the Model 188 came on September 25, 1957. Ansett's parent company purchased Australian National Airways on October 4, 1957, to form Ansett-ANA, with routes totaling more than 17,000 miles, covering the whole of Australia and Tasmania.

The actual contract for only two Electras was signed on December 9, 1958. Approval came from the Australian Government, which was heavily involved in the country's airline industry, directing purchase programs for not only Ansett but also TAA, QANTAS and Tasman Empire Airways, Ltd. (TEAL). Ansett's first Electra (msn 1039) was delivered on February 27, 1959, and began Melbourne– Sydney service on March 10. The second aircraft (msn 1047) arrived one month later. These Electras were delivered with 60 tourist and 18 first-class seats.

As the first two Electras entered service, Ansett successfully petitioned the government for permission to order a third (msn 1044) in November 1959, to be delivered the following February. The fleet maintained reliable passenger service for over a decade, even with the arrival of Ansett's first Boeing 727 in late 1964.

The early 1970s saw a change in the Electra's role when three aircraft were flown back to California for conversion by Lockheed Aircraft Service Company to Model 188AF freighter configurations. The cost of these modifications was approximately $800,000 per aircraft; the last makeover was completed in October 1972.

Ansett's Electra freighters proved to be so efficient that in August 1974 the airline purchased a similarly modified, ex-American Airlines aircraft (msn 1123). It was operated for slightly less than three years before being sold. The original three Electras soldiered on until finally disposed of in mid-1984. The crews of these turboprops wore a wombat symbol, recognizing that they flew principally at night.

Of the original purchasing airlines, Ansett-ANA proved to be the longest running Electra operator.

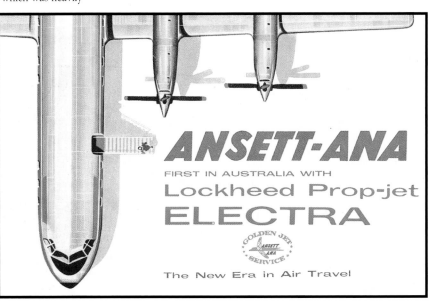

ANSETT-ANA
FIRST IN AUSTRALIA WITH
Lockheed Prop-jet
ELECTRA
The New Era in Air Travel

	ANSETT-ANA	
	(All built as 188As)	
msn	*Registration*	*Notes*
1039	VH-RMA	Converted to 188AF; July 1972
1044	VH-RMC	Operated by Lockheed for avionics tests as N1883, November 1959 to February 1960. Converted to 188AF; May 1972
1047	VH-RMB	Converted to 188AF; October 1972
1123	VH-RMG	Originally American Airlines, N6132A Converted to 188AF; August 1975

VH-RMA pauses at Oakland in February 1959, on its delivery flight to Australia. (Larry Smalley; Henry Tenby Collection)

VH-RMB at Melbourne in 1971, following cargo conversion. (Peter J. Sweeten)

VH-RMA in its final colors. Note the wombat symbol below the cockpit windows. (Karsten Heiligtag; Jon Proctor Collection)

N9701C in delivery colors. (Lockheed Martin Corporation)

Braniff International Airways

Dating back to 1928, Braniff had been associated with shorter routes covering the central United States. After World War II, the airline began expanding its system to include the breadth of the United States and, later, Central and South America. In the early 1950s, company managers began searching for an aircraft to replace the piston-engine fleet, then an assortment of DC-3s, DC-6s and -7Cs, plus Convair-Liners. The desired replacement was an aircraft that would be efficient over short-haul legs but still suitable for new, longer runs. After settling on the 188, an order for nine was announced on December 16, 1955, with the actual contract signed on February 20, 1956.

Braniff began turboprop service on June 15, 1959, over the San Antonio–Dallas–New York and Houston–Dallas–Chicago routes. By year's end, Washington-National, Denver and Colorado Springs had become Electra destinations. Flights to Kansas City and Minneapolis-St. Paul began in early 1960, and Mexico City in November. The 188 was gradually

introduced to more airports, until it became a regular visitor at most of Braniff's North American destinations.

A tenth Electra (msn 1134) from an abandoned Capital Airlines order was delivered on May 10, 1962. Finally in October 1966, Braniff leased an eleventh aircraft (msn 1004) for a period of one year to increase capacity.

Harding Lawrence, who took the helm of Braniff International on April 1, 1965, thought that his airline was a least 10 years behind the industry in terms of public perception. This belief had two major impacts on the Electra. First was the association between Braniff, Lawrence, and his wife, advertising executive Mary Wells. At the helm of the prestigious ad agency Wells-Rich-Greene, she was commissioned by Lawrence to bring Braniff out of its perceived old-fashioned image. The well-known result was termed the "End of the Plain Plane," featuring airliners – including the Electra – painted in an assortment of "jelly bean" colors. To Lawrence, all this was a calculated risk; nonetheless, Braniff became the darling of the advertising industry.

Unfortunately for the Electra, Lawrence's second immediate goal was what has become known as "fleet rationalization." He did not like Braniff's amalgamation of airliners including, among others, the Boeing 707, BAC 1-11 and Electra. Lawrence proclaimed that Braniff would become an all-Boeing airline, although in the end, this did not occur.

The Electra's demise at the carrier began on March 28, 1968. The fleet was sold as a whole to Citizens National Bank and leased back for one more year – until March 27, 1969, then withdrawn and turned over to the new owners.

An original Electra with Braniff markings greets the new version during delivery ceremonies at Love Field, Dallas. (Todd Duhnke Collection)

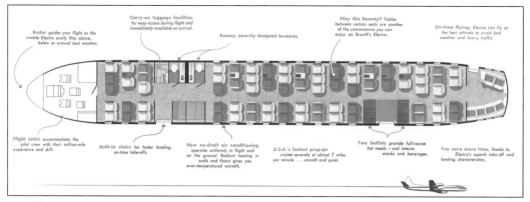

Braniff's unique floor plan alternated four- and five-abreast seating. (Jon Proctor Collection)

BRANIFF INTERNATIONAL AIRWAYS

msn	Registration	Model
1040	N9701C	188A
1052	N9702C	188A
1067	N9703C	188A
1086	N9704C	188A
1090	N9705C	188A
1095	N9706C	188A
1099	N9707C	188A
1106	N9708C	188A
1114	N9709C	188A
1134	N9710C	188C*

* from Capital Airlines order

Leased Aircraft

1004	N16816	188A

(from F. B. Ayer)

Looking aft from mid-cabin. Note the aft lounge wall decoration. (Todd Duhnke Collection)

N9701C, photographed in 1972, shortly after sale to Universal Trading Corporation. (Harry Sievers Collection)

Reflecting the "end of the plain plane," Braniff Electras in various shades (top to bottom):
N9704C. (Manuel Delgado)
N9709C. (Manuel Delgado)
N9710C. (Leon Franco; Henry Tenby Collection)

N5501, first of a 40-strong fleet. (Lockheed Martin Corporation)

Eastern Air Lines

Eastern's president Eddie Rickenbacker was nervous about the inevitable arrival of the turbine age, demonstrated by his reluctance to order the new jets. One thing Rickenbacker did know was that in 1955 his aging piston fleet needed updating. At a time when other airlines were plunging into jet purchases, Rickenbacker ordered 40 DC-7s. Simultaneously, he made a foray into the world of turbine-powered airliners by purchasing 40 Lockheed Electras.

The combined cost of 80 propeller-driven aircraft, plus a modification program on existing Super Constellations, was more than twice the amount Eastern had in the budget for jets. Many thought this large outlay for propliners was a ploy to delay investing in jet equipment. However, as wary Rickenbacker might have been about jets, he was quite enthusiastic about the Electra, which would allow Eastern to both modernize its fleet and remain competitive while other airlines were breaking in pure jets.

Eastern's post-LEAP 188s were called "Super Electras." N5532 wears the carrier's second Electra livery. (Terry Waddington)

When company managers examined the original Lockheed design, they liked the idea but wanted more payload and increased range. Their ideas, combined with those of American and Lockheed, brought about the final Model 188 design. Eastern announced its Electra order on September 27, 1955; formal contract signing came on February 9, 1956. Its aircraft would be equipped with 66 first-class seats plus six in the aft lounge. Corporate thinking was that when the company received jet equipment, the Electras would be reconfigured to an all-coach layout and assigned to secondary routes. Options on 30 additional 188s were never converted.

Eastern took delivery of the first production Electra (msn 1007) on October 8, 1958. After dealing with a similar pilot dilemma faced at American Airlines, it became the first airline to introduce the type into scheduled revenue service. On January 12, 1959, the inaugural 188 flight departed Miami at 9:30 a.m. with 20 paying passengers on board. After a brief stop at New York-Idlewild it continued to Montreal. This first flight was delayed in New York with a generator problem that was fixed in less than one hour. On the same morning, two additional Electra services departed from New York for Miami. A week later, with a fleet of 12 aircraft, Eastern's 188s were also serving Tampa, San Antonio, Detroit, Chicago, Cleveland, Atlanta, Washington D.C. and Newark; service to San Juan began the following month.

The economical airliner quickly proved popular with passengers and employees alike. In particular, hometown-rival National Airlines and its DC-7s were being out-performed by the Electra, although National would soon turn the tables with its introduction of jet equipment.

Rickenbacker believed that the industry transition from props to jets would last longer than it actually did, but Eastern's DC-8s brought the airline into the jet age by January 1960. However, the two airliners that eventually demoted the carrier's Electras were the Boeing 727 and the Douglas DC-9, which entered service in 1964 and 1966, respectively.

It was a natural progression that 188s began replacing Lockheed Constellations on Eastern's Air-Shuttle which had been in operation since April 1961. With an ever-growing short- to medium-haul jet fleet, Eastern's Electras eventually became redundant on both the main routes and the Shuttle, prompting a sell-off that began in 1968. By May 1974 the fleet was down to thirteen 188s, which served solely as backups to jets on the Shuttle. The last turboprop Shuttle flights took place on October 31, 1977. The final Electra was disposed of in 1978.

msn	Registration	Model	msn	Registration	Model
		EASTERN AIR LINES			
1005	N5501	188A	1033	N5522	188A
1007	N5502	188A	1034	N5523	188A
1008	N5503	188A	1036	N5524	188A
1009	N5504	188A	1038	N5525	188A
1010	N5505	188A	1042	N5526	188A
1011	N5506	188A	1043	N5527	188A
1012	N5507	188A	1045	N5528	188A
1013	N5509	188A	1048	N5529	188A
1014	N5510	188A	1053	N5530	188A
1016	N5511	188A	1055	N5531	188A
1017	N5512	188A	1060	N5532	188A
1018	N5513	188A	1062	N5533	188A
1020	N5514	188A	1066	N5534	188A
1021	N5515	188A	1068	N5535	188A
1022	N5516	188A	1071	N5536	188C
1023	N5517	188A	1075	N5537	188C
1026	N5518	188A	1078	N5538	188C
1029	N5519	188A	1080	N5539	188C
1030	N5520	188A	1088	N5540	188C
1032	N5521	188A	1098	N5541	188C

The Air-Shuttle
EASTERN

N5531 in Eastern's "Hockey Stick" colors at New York's LaGuardia Airport while operating the Air-Shuttle. It was destroyed on the ground by a bomb in 1976. (Bryant Petitt, Jr. Collection)

PK-GLB was christened *Tjandi Bororudur*. (Lockheed Martin Corporation)

Garuda Indonesian Airways

Garuda was formed in March 1950 as the national airline of Indonesia; by the end of the decade it was flying a fleet of aging DC-3s and Convair 340s. In order to compete on longer international routes to destinations such as Tokyo and Hong Kong, the airline purchased three 188Cs, all of which were delivered in January 1961. Electra service began in March. Garuda lost one aircraft (msn 2021) in a crash at Manado, Indonesia, on February 2, 1967.

GARUDA INDONESIAN AIRWAYS		
(All built as 188Cs)		
msn	Registration	Name
2020	PK-GLA	*Palau Bali*
2021	PK-GLB	*Tjandi Bororudur*
2022	PK-GLC	*Danau Toba*

The remaining two continued in service until 1972 and then were parked in open storage at Jakarta, until sold to California Airmotive Corporation the following year.

Allison Division of General Motors

The Electra's engines were manufactured by the Allison Division of General Motors. In order to continue the test and development of these 501 D13 power plants, Allison took delivery of the sixth Electra (msn 1006 – N5501V) on July 10, 1958, and flew it in varying capacities for more than three years. It was sold to the Los Angeles Dodgers Baseball Club on November 22, 1961.
(Lockheed Martin Corporation)

PH-LLA also wears Lockheed "dealer plate" registration N6934C below the aft windows. (Lockheed Martin Corporation)

KLM-Royal Dutch Airlines

In the late 1950s, KLM was looking for turbine aircraft to replace its piston fleet. Already a Viscount 802 operator, the airline sought an airliner with the increased range needed to reach Middle Eastern and Far Eastern destinations. Settling on the Electra for this role, KLM signed a contract for twelve 188Cs on February 29, 1956, and announced this purchase a week later. The aircraft were to be configured for 67 passengers without the aft lounge.

The first of KLM's Electras (msn 2001) was handed over on September 21, 1959. Deliveries continued on a regular basis until the last one (msn 2019) was handed over on December 14, 1960. Service was inaugurated on December 9, 1959, from Amsterdam to several European cities including Dusseldorf, Vienna, Frankfurt and Budapest, plus destinations in the Middle East. Later a flight schedule to Singapore (with stops) was added.

The only European operator of factory delivered 188s, KLM found its new turboprops to be well-suited for its intended short- and medium-haul routes. They proved to be as fast in schedule speed as competing Caravelles and were superior in performance during winter months with its ability to handle bad weather and icy runways. In addition, the Electra fleet exceeded all other KLM types in on-time performance.

The fate of KLM's Electra fleet rested with the arrival of Douglas DC-9s starting in April 1966. As the Douglas jetliner was put on-line, the 188 began to replace Viscounts on KLM's shorter routes. By 1968 the entire Electra fleet – reduced to 11 following the crash of PH-LLM in 1961 – was up for sale. Two (msns 2009 and 2014) were leased briefly to Martinair Holland before the 11 airframes were purchased by Universal Airlines for conversion to freighters. The first aircraft was relinquished on March 14, 1968. On February 2, 1969, Universal took delivery of the final KLM Electra.

Msn 2003, named *Venus,* at London-Heathrow, in August 1965. Note the round-tip Hamilton Standard props and modified tail livery. (Terry Waddington)

KLM-Royal Dutch Airlines

(All built as 188Cs and equipped with Hamilton-Standard propellers)

msn	Registration	Name
2001	PH-LLA	*Mercurius*
2003	PH-LLB	*Venus*
2006	PH-LLC	*Mars*
2009	PH-LLD	*Jupiter*
2012	PH-LLE	*Saturnus*
2013	PH-LLF	*Uranus*
2014	PH-LLG	*Neptunus*
2015	PH-LLH	*Pluto*
2016	PH-LLI	*Ceres*
2017	PH-LLK	*Pallas*
2018	PH-LLL	*Orion*
2019	PH-LLM	*Sirius*

The original National "Airline of the Stars" livery is worn by msn 1035 in this pre-delivery pose. (Lockheed Martin Corporation)

National Airlines

Like that of rival Eastern Air Lines, National's route system was principally centered in the southeastern United States; it consisted of short-to-medium-length legs with a few longer runs up the Eastern Seaboard. This route structure, serviced with an aging fleet of piston-powered airliners and lacking a suitable jet replacement, made the Electra a perfect choice. The airline signed up for 12 on December 9, 1955, announcing its order on January 3, 1956. This made National the first airline to buy the 188, beating American Airlines by six days. Although the order included 23 options, the fleet number eventually stabilized at 14. Aircraft interior configurations included 72 passenger seats (54 first-class and 18 coach) plus the aft lounge. Three additional 188s were later purchased from American Airlines.

National took delivery of its first Electra (msn 1035) on April 1, 1959, and began turboprop service April 23 on the New York–Miami run. The last two airplanes from the reduced order were delivered in January 1961, followed by the three ex-American aircraft in November 1962. The Electra was used throughout the National system until arrival of the first long-haul jet equipment in 1960. The type was then relegated mostly to shorter routes, although it served on longer flights to the West Coast when these new routes were initiated in 1961.

Although National's Boeing 727s began arriving in October 1964, the company's first Electra was not sold until January 1968. All were gone by the following December.

		NATIONAL AIRLINES *(All built as 188As)*			
msn	*Registration*	*Fleet Number*	*msn*	*Registration*	*Fleet Number*
1027	N5016K	66 (ex-American)	1089	N5007K	57
1031	N5017K	67 (ex-American)	1092	N5008K	58
1035	N5001K	51	1096	N5009K	59
1054	N5015K	65 (ex-American)	1097	N5010K	60
1059	N5002K	52	1104	N5011K	61
1064	N5003K	53	1107	N5012K	62
1076	N5004K	54	1146	N5013K	63
1079	N5005K	55	1148	N5014K	64
1084	N5006K	56			

A later livery seen on N5016K – a former American 188A – at Philadelphia in 1968. (Bruce Drum)

N121US, first of the original order for 10 Electras; eight options were firmed up later. (Lockheed Martin Corporation)

Northwest Airlines

Northwest Airlines marked its jet age entry with an $83-million financing package for the purchase of both Lockheed Electras and Douglas DC-8s. The airline announced its purchase of ten 188s on May 1, 1958, and signed the contract on November 26; the cost was approximately $2.4 million per aircraft.

The first long-range "C" Model (msn 1057) was delivered on July 19, 1959, and by December the order was complete. Revenue Electra service began September 1, on the New York–Milwaukee–Minneapolis-St. Paul, New York–Seattle and Chicago–Minneapolis runs.

Foregoing the aft lounge, these aircraft were configured in mixed first-class/coach configurations.

Northwest operated the Electra over medium-haul routes such as Chicago–Miami and New York–Minneapolis-St. Paul while also taking advantage of its long-range capabilities on nonstops between New York and Seattle. NWA was the only airline to fly 188s on transcontinental nonstop segments. The type met with immediate success for the company and the traveling public. During the first month of operation, Northwest's turboprops averaged greater than 80-percent load factors. Options on an additional 18 Electras were placed on October 17, 1959, but only eight were taken up, and delivered between March and June 1961.

The purchase of Boeing 727s in 1964 soon relegated the 188 to shorter routes, characterized by multiple legs and rapid turnarounds, both of which were the Electra's forte. As the 727 became more prevalent, the inevitable 188 sell-off began, starting in September 1966. The last two left Northwest in September 1971.

NORTHWEST AIRLINES (All built as 188Cs)	
msn	Registration
1057	N121US
1077	N122US
1082	N123US
1085	N124US
1101	N125US
1105	N126US
1108	N127US
1111	N128US
1112	N129US
1113	N130US
1131	N131US
1132	N132US
1137	N133US
1138	N134US
1139	N135US
1141	N136US
1142	N137US
1144	N138US

N135US in June 1968, without tail insignia. (J. Roger Bentley)

Advertised as the "Electra JET," PSA's first was N171PS. (Lockheed Martin Corporation)

Pacific Southwest Airlines

Pacific Southwest Airlines (PSA) epitomized service over short routes, combined with multiple, quick turnarounds. Founded by Kenneth Friedkin, PSA concentrated on high-density, high-frequency California intrastate flights. To Friedkin, it was obvious that long-range jets were not a viable choice. Although he did announce his intention to order two French Sud Aviation Caravelles in 1957, the deal was never completed. With its designed efficiency over the short haul, the 188 was perfect for the job. A contract for three was signed on September 16, 1957, and the announcement of the $8 million deal came five days later. PSA's airframes were actually leased from the Baron Hilton's Electrahilt Corporation while the engines were leased directly from Allison.

	PACIFIC SOUTHWEST AIRLINES	
msn	*Registration*	*Notes*
1001	N174PA	188A
1028	N6106A	ex-American Airlines 188A
		Lake Tahoe service April 1975 to April 1979
1072	N6118A	ex-American Airlines 188A
		Lake Tahoe service 1977 to February 1979
1091	N171PS	188C, Lake Tahoe service August 1975 to
		February 1979
1109	N172PS	188C
1110	N173PS	188C
1121	N6130A	ex-American Airlines 188A
		Lake Tahoe service October 1975 to
		February 1979
1130	N175PS	188C, from Capital Airlines order
1133	N376PS	ex-Sports Aloft, Inc. 188C, from
		Capital Airlines order

The first two Electras (msns 1091 and 1109) were delivered on November 6 and November 30, 1959, respectively. One month later, the third 188 arrived in San Diego. PSA ordered these aircraft equipped with 92 coach seats, while retaining the aft six-passenger lounge, for a total capacity of 98. Entering service in December between San Diego and San Francisco (both nonstop and via Los Angeles or Burbank), the Electra proved to be quite popular with travelers. Flight times were significantly reduced below that of the DC-4s the new turboprops replaced, and frequencies were increased.

With load factors on the rise, PSA acquired three additional Electras starting in 1961. The company's final 188 was the last unsold aircraft still remaining in Lockheed's inventory, left over from the Capital order.

Even though the first Boeing 727-14s began arriving in April 1965, the 188 continued as a valuable fleet member. However, with the December 1967 delivery of the first stretched Boeing 727-214, both the Electras and 727-14s were slated for retirement. Electra phase-out occurred between February 1968 and March 1969.

PSA became reacquainted with turboprops in 1975 when the Electra entered service to Lake Tahoe. Since 727s were not allowed to fly into this resort's airport, PSA leased four 188s, including one of its former fleet (msn 1091). Tahoe service ended in early 1979, as did PSA's association with the type; the last aircraft was retired in April 1979.

Electra titles were deleted in the modified colors worn on N175PS, photographed at San Francisco International in November 1967. (Terry Coxall)

N6130A, seen at the Lake Tahoe Airport in November 1976, wearing a three-tone livery. (Harry Sievers Collection)

Ex-American Airlines 188 N6118A reflects PSA's final Electra markings. (Lockheed Martin Corporation)

VH-ECB, *Pacific Explorer.* (Lockheed Martin Corporation)

QANTAS Empire Airways

The Australian Government exercised a firm hand in the equipment acquisition programs of the country's airlines. This policy applied not only to the domestic airlines but also to QANTAS Empire Airways (originally Queensland and Northern Territory Aerial Services), Australia's overseas carrier.

Although the government was leaning more towards a British manufacturer, QANTAS was allowed to order four Lockheed Electras on April 1, 1958. The turboprops would be used on short-haul international segments, while a Boeing 707 order would fulfill longer overseas routes. All four 188Cs were delivered during the last two months of 1959.

Seating 59 in a mixed-class layout, QANTAS Electra service began December 18, 1959, on flights to Tokyo via Manila. The 188C was also used for flights to

QANTAS		
(All built as 188Cs)		
msn	**Registration**	**Name**
2002	VH-ECA	*Pacific Electra*
2004	VH-ECB	*Pacific Explorer*
2007	VH-ECC	*Pacific Endeavour*
2008	VH-ECD	*Pacific Enterprise*

and from Noumea, New Guinea, New Zealand, Johannesburg (South Africa), and points in the Far East.

With a lack of domestic runs, the Electra's primary usefulness was lost when more 707s were delivered by the mid-1960s. The first 188 to go was msn 2007, sold to Air New Zealand in April 1965. Two more (msns 2002 and 2004) were sold to Air California in June and August 1976. The last aircraft (msn 2008) went to Nomads, Inc. in April 1971.

Tasman Empire Airways
(Air New Zealand since April 1965)

At the time Tasman Empire Airways, Ltd. (TEAL) purchased its first Electra, the company was jointly owned by the New Zealand and Australian governments. Originally looking at both the de Havilland Comet and Convair 880, the airline was allowed to purchase three long-range 188Cs, and an order was placed on September 5, 1958. This controversial decision was felt to have been dictated by the Australian influence and brought about the expression "TEAL: Take Electras and like it!" Only a few years later, in 1961, New Zealand obtained complete ownership of its flag carrier.

ZK-TEA on a pre-delivery photo flight with dual U.S. and New Zealand registrations. (Lockheed Martin Corporation)

ZK-TEA wearing dual QANTAS/ANZ titles in September 1971.
(via B. Dannecker)

TEAL's first Electra (msn 2005) arrived on October 15, 1959, followed two months later by the second and third aircraft (msns 2010 and 2011). Revenue flights began on December 1, 1959, over the Auckland–Sydney route. Flights to Fiji commenced the following month.

Even with the introduction of DC-8 jet equipment in March 1965, TEAL – which became Air New Zealand a month later – continued to utilize 188s. It acquired an ex-QANTAS aircraft to replace msn 2011, previously written off in a training accident. A second former QANTAS Electra was leased from 1970 for use on Auckland–Sydney joint services with the Australian carrier.

One of the 188Cs was sold off in 1968, and another left in 1971. The last two, including the first received, were sold in May 1972.

VH-TLA in a short-lived color scheme. (Lockheed Martin Corporation)

Trans-Australia Airlines

Another "down under" Electra operator was government-owned Trans-Australia Airlines (TAA), a domestic carrier. Having operated Vickers Viscounts since late 1954, the airline's leadership felt that the Caravelle would usher it firmly into the jet age. However, Australian government officials had different ideas, believing that the state of the country's airports and navigational facilities precluded jet operations.

Although they wanted a British airliner, lawmakers allowed purchase of the Lockheed Electra. The government had such a tight rein on these airlines that Ansett-ANA was forced to relinquish two of its 188 delivery positions to TAA in order to balance competition.

The last of TAA's factory delivered Electras, VH-TLC wears an updated livery as seen in this August 1960 photo. (Lockheed Martin Corporation)

On June 15, 1959, TAA General Manager John Ryland accepted the airline's first Electra (msn 1061). The airliner was equipped with 68 seats plus the aft lounge. Service began July 7 on the Melbourne–Adelaide–Perth run and a few days later over the Melbourne–Sydney–Brisbane route. TAA's second aircraft (msn 1069) was delivered on July 26, 1959.

The competition between TAA and rival Ansett-ANA was so fierce that when Ansett was allowed to order an additional Electra, TAA also demanded and received permission to buy one more as well. Its third (msn 1147) began service in September 1960. A fourth and final Electra (msn 2008) was leased new from QANTAS between December 1959 and September 1960.

Although TAA began service with the Boeing 727 in November 1964 and the Douglas DC-9 in April 1967, the 188s remained until 1972 when they were sold en masse.

Fly TAA ELECTRA Mk. Ⅱ

and enjoy the benefits of TAA Airmanship

VH-TLC, photographed in February 1970, reflects yet another variation of TAA's markings. (James Bell)

Western's first Electra, N7135C. (Lockheed Martin Corporation)

Western Airlines

Western's 1955 Annual Report states that the airline was actively seeking a suitable new airliner for its route system. Although WAL President Terrell Drinkwater wanted to quickly retire the DC-3s and DC-4s, he was astounded at the price of a single jet airliner and hesitated at the purchase. Some executives at Western thought the airline should go right to jets and not waste time with turboprops. However, Drinkwater believed the Lockheed Electra would fit nicely in the role of a short-to-medium-range airliner while remaining profitable on the occasional long haul. Western signed a contract for nine Lockheed Electras on May 14, 1956.

The first (msn 1046) was delivered on May 20, 1959, and inaugurated revenue flying on August 1 between the West Coast cities of Los Angeles, San Francisco, Portland and Seattle. Two months later, Electra service was initiated over Western's mountain routes, to Salt Lake City, Denver and Minneapolis.

The turboprop garnered praise from crews, passengers and Western's accounting office. Early 188 interiors, designed by Henry Dreyfuss, were equipped with 66 first-class seats and the aft lounge.

The only group at Western that had a problem with the Electra was the flight attendant corps (stewardesses, back then). Lockheed-designed galleys had been created by male engineers, and not considered to be user friendly by the all-female cabin staff. After a review by engineers, management and a panel of flight attendants, a new galley was proposed and adopted. In addition to improving life for the cabin staff, the updated Electra equipment became standardized throughout the Western fleet, reducing inventories and maintenance costs.

By the close of 1959, Western had taken delivery of its first five 188s and placed an order for three more, bringing the planned fleet up to a total of 12. The airline paid around $2.5 million per unit. Later deliveries contained a high-density, 96 seat all-coach (no lounge) arrangement.

Western began pure-jet service over the same Los Angeles–Seattle route with two 707-139s (leased from Boeing) on June 1, 1960; company-

presenting Electra/JET

A TOTALLY NEW DIMENSION IN JET-AGE TRAVEL

WESTERN AIRLINES

owned Boeing 720-047Bs would follow in April 1961. However, the Electra was not replaced, but instead reassigned to the shorter routes, replacing DC-6Bs.

With the success of Western's first jets, Drinkwater changed his thinking and in 1963 sent his staff looking for a suitable Electra

In colors updated to match its Boeing 720B fleet, N7142C on taxi-in at West Yellowstone Airport in August 1967. (Robert D. Archer)

replacement. The BAC 1-11 and DC-9 were considered front runners, but he agreed to wait for a time and ultimately Western bought both the Boeing 737 and the 727, delivered in 1968 and 1969, respectively. Unlike many Electra operators, Western did not sell off its fleet when introducing new shorter-range jets and kept the turboprops beyond a planned 1966 retirement.

On May 3, 1969, the airline announced that it would modify five Electras into combination passenger/freighter airliners. They would be used on the Alaska route network, acquired as a result of the October 1, 1967, merger with Pacific Northern Airlines (PNA). The 188 replaced PNA's Constellations. In addition, three more Electras were modified to all-cargo configurations for use throughout the Western system. Work began in July 1968 and was completed by the end of January 1969 at a cost of $4 million.

As the Boeing jet fleet grew larger, Western's Electras became redundant. The four remaining all-passenger aircraft were withdrawn in 1969 and sold to a leasing company a year later. The last eight were then gradually disposed of, with the final two sold to Nordic Air in August 1972.

WESTERN AIRLINES _(All built as 188As)_			
msn	Registration	Model	Fleet
1046	N7135C	188A	#135
1070	N7136C	188A	#136
1074	N7137C	188A	#137
1087	N7138C	188A	#138
1094	N7139C	188A	#139. Modified to 188PF
1118	N7140C	188A	#140. Modified to 188PF
1127	N7141C	188A	#141. Modified to 188PF
1128	N7142C	188A	#142. Modified to 188PF
1129	N7143C	188A	#143. Modified to 188AF
1140	N9744C	188A	#144. Modified to 188PF
1143	N9745C	188A	#145. Modified to 188AF
1145	N9746C	188A	#146. Modified to 188AF

N7140C in storage at Las Vegas. The 188A was converted to a Combi; note Alaska's state flag on the tail. (Terry Waddington)

Artist's rendering of Capital's originally proposed Electra color scheme. (Lockheed Martin Corporation)

Capital Airlines

Several other airlines expressed interest in purchasing factory-new Electras, but Capital Airlines deserves mention because of its long-term relationship with the Electra project even while never having flown one. An October 1959 announcement stated that the airline had financial backing to order five Electras even though it was having difficulty paying for its Vickers Viscounts.

THE CAPITAL AIRLINES ORDER		
(All built as 188Cs)		
msn	Registration	Ultimate Operator
1130	N181H	U.S. Navy, then PSA
1133	N182H	Sports Aloft, then PSA
1134	N183H	Braniff
1135	N184H	Sports Aloft, then American Flyers
1136	N185H	Sports Aloft, then American Flyers

Nevertheless Lockheed reserved five positions on the assembly line for the order. Capital's ability to pay for these Electras became moot once United Air Lines began to look at acquiring the company. Even before to the actual June 1, 1961, merger of Capital and United, the Electra order was canceled. Lockheed then sold the aircraft to other customers.

Awaiting propellers, msn 1133 on the Burbank ramp in Capital's final livery. The Electra went briefly to Sports Aloft before finding a home with PSA as N376PS. (Lockheed Martin Corporation)

Sports Aloft

Sports Aloft specialized in charters carrying sports teams. In February 1962 the firm purchased three new Electras from the defunct Capital Airlines order, and some work was completed to Sports Aloft's specifications. Lockheed was forced to repossess the airliners for non-payment in December 1962 before any revenue Electra flights commenced.

SPORTS ALOFT, INC.		
(All built as 188Cs)		
msn	Registration	Ultimate Buyer
1133	N181H	(original registration N182H); to PSA
1135	N182H	American Flyers
1136	N183H	American Flyers

Lockheed Aircraft Corporation

Lockheed operated four prototype Electras in a variety of evaluation and certification roles. The first two were used primarily for flight testing and certification. Lockheed operated Ship One until April 19, 1961, when it was handed over to PSA. Ship Two was delivered to Cathay Pacific on June 29, 1959.

The third Electra prototype was used initially by Lockheed as a static test airframe, then converted to the prototype P-3 Orion and accepted by the U.S. Navy on September 18, 1962.

In addition to its test and evaluation duties, Ship Four was also a company demonstrator. Wearing N7144C (re-registered from N1884), this aircraft flew on a world sales tour in late 1958. Shortly thereafter, it was sold to Cathay Pacific.

In addition to the four prototypes, Lockheed operated several airframes prior to customer delivery. The aircraft were used for testing various systems and not modified to any great extent. Lockheed also retained ownership of several Electras that were primarily for lease or the result of undelivered or canceled orders.

LOCKHEED AIRCRAFT CORPORATION

msn	Registration	Notes
9999	N/A	Operational fuselage used for destructive testing
1001	N1881	188A - First Prototype
1002	N1882	188A
1003	N1883	188A - Static test airframe. Converted to YP-3A Orion
1004	N1884	188A - World tour demonstrator, re-registered N1744C

AIRCRAFT OPERATED BY LOCKHEED PRIOR TO DELIVERY

msn	Registration	Notes
1103	N9725C	188C - Originally to Hughes Tool Company, not delivered; to FAA
1079	N5005K	188A - South America sales tour; to National
2001	N6934C	188C - Flight testing; to KLM
2005	N9724C	188C - Instrument testing;. to TEAL

Turboprop Versus Pure-Jet

Over the production span of an airliner several "break-even" points are often predicted by the manufacturer, to identify the number of aircraft sales required to turn a profit. Usually starting out small and increasing with costs, these numbers are closely monitored. It was first estimated that the Electra would break even at around 190 airplanes, but in the end the number had risen to 300.

Production was halted after only 170 were built, not exactly a long run and certainly not enough for Lockheed to come close to the original break-even number. The financial loss has been estimated at more than $25 million, however this figure does not include the profit earned by the P-3 Orion program.

During the 1960s, the Electra's short-to-medium-range, turboprop airliner role – to which it was particularly well-suited – had no serious rivals. In the beginning, its order book filled quite rapidly, so what then caused the premature termination of the program?

First of all, there was a series of disastrous crashes (see Chapter III) that tainted the airplane's image, although a successful re-engineering program caused this perception to fade with time. Also, some of the original airlines – American and Eastern in particular – over-ordered the Electra in the first place. However, the primary reason for the early cessation of the program was the introduction of the equally capable pure-jet airliners in this class, namely the Boeing 727, the Douglas DC-9, and later, the Boeing 737. These aircraft were still years away when the Electra first flew, but with the apparent success of the Boeing 707 and the Douglas DC-8, many formerly cautious airline executives thought that pure jets were the industry's future.

No longer worried, they decided to forego the turboprop phase and transition straight to jets. Several Electra operators rapidly switched to jets, while others kept the type for several years; PSA, Eastern (on the Shuttle) and Ansett are examples of the latter group. As the original operators sold off 188s, other airlines found the Electra a perfect fleet addition and a brisk market of pre-owned Electras began to develop.

Msn 1001, the first prototype Electra. (Lockheed Martin Corporation)

As the first of 35 Electras for American Airlines, N6101A was a very photogenic airliner. Unfortunately, it crashed only 11 days after entering service. (Lockheed Martin Corporation)

Safety engineering was paramount to Lockheed managers in the Electra design. Their new airliner had the newest concepts in "fail safe" airframe construction, redundant systems, an enormous amount of surplus power and the latest safety devices. It quickly became the desired aircraft in its niche, preferred by airlines and passengers alike as a fast, comfortable and profitable machine. However, shortly after this grand start, the Electra experienced a series of crashes that might well have doomed the series to extinction.

February 3, 1959; American Flight 320 (msn 1015 – N6101A)

American Airlines' *Flagship New York* was just over two months old when it crashed on approach to New York's LaGuardia Airport. Flight 320 departed from Chicago-Midway Airport at 9 p.m. On board the nonstop flight were three cockpit crew members, two flight attendants and 68 passengers. LaGuardia weather was reported as "measured (ceiling) four hundred (feet) overcast, two miles visibility," slightly above the prescribed approach minimums for Runway 22. Although some aircraft ahead of Flight 320 had missed the approach, conditions were still legal and within the capabilities of Captain Albert DeWitt, his crew and the Electra.

At 11:53 p.m. Flight 320 passed the New Rochelle navigation fix and the control tower instructed the crew to report passing the LaGuardia radio range. Having reported passing this fix (2.8 miles from the runway) Flight 320 was cleared to land. Seven seconds later *Flagship New York* crashed into the East River 4,891 feet short of the threshold. The first officer, flight engineer, one flight attendant and five passengers survived; 65 others lost their lives. The majority of the aircraft components were recovered from the river and after examination were found to be operating at the time of the crash.

The Civil Aeronautics Board (CAB) investigation concluded that the accident was caused by "a premature descent below landing minimums." Several witness accounts and a review of the aircraft's flight path indicated that Flight 320 passed over the LaGuardia radio range between 300 and 500 feet. The required crossing altitude is 820 feet. In addition, the Electra passed the station in a constant rate of descent which it maintained until impact. First Officer Frank Hlavacek stated that the

captain was using the autopilot to control the aircraft. In addition to citing a faulty approach technique, the Board highlighted several novel aspects of the Electra that, combined with the crew's lack of experience in a new airliner, may have been contributing causes of the accident. Of particular interest were the altimeters.

A dual altimeter failure was examined and rejected. A single altimeter failure on the Captain's side was also considered although a definite conclusion was not reached. More plausible was the fact that these instruments were of a new type. They replaced the more familiar multiple needle indicators with a single needle and a drum arrangement. The readings may have been misinterpreted during the descent.

Another instrument, the vertical speed indicator (VSI), although similar to previous types, had a different scale on the gauge face. The Board noted that a 90-degree downward displacement of the VSI needle – on gauges of airliners the crew had previously flown – would indicate a 750-foot-per-minute rate of descent, reasonable for an instrument approach. However on the Electra, this same displacement equated to a 2,300-foot-per-minute rate. The Board conjectured that a pilot preoccupied with a high workload instrument approach could have misread both the altimeter and the VSI and not correctly determined the altitude and the descent rate. In this case, the aircraft was allowed to fly itself into the East River.

In the end, the CAB ruled that the accident cause was pilot error with several cumulative factors. The ruling incensed Captain DeWitt's fellow pilots at American, who believed he was deceived by the new equipment. Although this debate raged on, several suggestions were put forth to prevent a similar occurrence. The CAB imposed a temporary increase in weather minimums for the Electra, until the new altimeters were replaced with the older type. A review of autopilot approach techniques was also mandated. Believing that a simulator program would have helped prevent this accident, the CAB continued its call for this type of training. Finally, the Board adopted an amendment to the Civil Air Regulations requiring the installation of Flight Data Recorders on turbine-powered airliners.

Despite the timing of this crash – so soon after the Electra's public introduction – the airplane itself was not subject to much doubt by the industry or the traveling public. In their eyes it was still a safe and productive airliner.

Tail of crashed Braniff N9705C. (Todd Duhnke Collection)

Whirl Mode

September 29, 1959; Braniff Flight 542 (msn 1090 – N9705C)

Originating in Houston, Texas, Braniff's late evening Flight 542 was scheduled to make stops in Dallas and Washington D.C., en route to New York's Idlewild Airport, where it was to arrive at 6:20 the following morning.

The assigned Electra had been delivered to Braniff only 10 days earlier. At 10:37 p.m. (22 minutes late due to a generator problem) Flight 542 proceeded on course for the 41-minute leg to Dallas carrying six crew members and 28 passengers. Routine communications with both Air Traffic Control and Braniff company radio indicated the flight was progressing smoothly at its 15,000-foot cruising altitude. At approximately 11:09 p.m. the 188 broke up and plunged to the ground just southeast of Buffalo, Texas. There were no survivors.

At first glance the total destruction of this airplane seemed to preclude examination. Its wreckage distribution pattern, however, revealed several clues. From the first item found (a length of hydraulic line) the debris formed an ellipse almost 14,000 feet long. Along a generally straight axis, the next component found was the Number One propeller and reduction gearbox. Next were the left wing with the Number One and Number Two engines still attached, then the Number Four engine, left stabilizer and right outboard wing panel.

At the main crash site investigators found craters that separately contained the main fuselage, empennage and the Number Three engine. Tree damage in this area indicated that the wreckage generally fell vertically to earth. The pattern also indicated a gradual, in-flight break-up.

Developing this scenario, the CAB closely studied the reported weather along Flight 542's flight path. In general, it was fine with scattered clouds at 20,000 feet and 10-to-15 miles visibility. Conditions were not conducive to clear-air turbulence and the isolated Texas thunderstorms could be easily avoided. Pilots in the area reported no unusual weather.

Several witnesses saw a large fireball in the sky and heard what they likened to "the sound of thunder," "the roar of a jet plane breaking the sound barrier," and "a whooshing, screaming noise." These observers listened to tapes of various noises, then were asked which more closely resembled the sound they heard that night. Their answers indicated that the common perception of the noise created by the Braniff Electra was that of propellers at supersonic speed and the sound of a jet airplane.

Recovered wreckage was taken to a warehouse in Dallas for reconstruction. Every component was examined for defects, damage, stress, contamination and proper operation before the accident. Testing revealed no abnormalities other than those attributed to impact damage. Fire patterns on the airframe were random in nature and indicative of an intense, explosive flash fire rather than a long, continuous burn. Also, because none of the molten aluminum deposits found in the wreckage contained evidence of air stream influence, the CAB concluded an in-flight fire did not cause the breakup.

Since it was clear that the left wing was one of the first major airframe parts to break away, considerable effort was placed on its examination. The wing separated between the Number Two engine and the fuselage. The lower span-wise wing planks showed evidence of being bent upwards prior to breaking in tension, after which the fracture faces re-contacted at least three times. Conversely, the upper span-wise wing planks in the area of the separation were broken into small, irregular pieces as a result of high positive compression and upward-bending loads. Basically, the left wing "flapped" up and returned to its original position as many as three times before separating up and away from the fuselage.

The power plants were also subject to scrutiny. It appeared the Number One engine mounts had failed, allowing the propeller, gearbox, forward section of the engine and air inlet to fall away. The mounts revealed evidence of bending in multiple directions and, after breaking, repeated contact between the fracture faces. The wiring and fuel lines forward of the firewall showed similar breakage.

The CAB concluded that these portions of the Number One engine lurched within the nacelle assembly and broke loose from the wing. The remaining engines were heavily damaged but did not show the same type of failure. None of the Allison 501s provided any evidence of overspeed, propeller runaway or other operational failure. Regarding the Number One engine and the left wing, the CAB could not determine which broke loose first or whether the two separated at the same time.

By March 1960 the CAB had rejected breakup causes. These included structural failure due to fatigue, collision with another aircraft, evasive maneuvering, severe weather and turbulence, sabotage, and malfunctions of the control boost system and autopilot. At this point all the CAB acknowledged was that the Electra had broken up in flight; the cause was unknown.

March 17, 1960; Northwest Flight 710 (msn 1057 – N121US)

Following the loss of Braniff Flight 542, the airline industry did not seem overly concerned and Electras continued in revenue service. One was a 188C model operated by Northwest Airlines.

On March 17, 1960, N121US was assigned to operate as Flight 710 from Minneapolis to Miami, with an en route stop at Chicago's Midway Airport.

Northwest's N121US under construction at Lockheed, Burbank. (Todd Duhnke Collection)

Right wing of the crashed N121US. Note shattered appearance of the wing planks (left).
(Todd Duhnke Collection)

Aeroproducts propeller from N121US. (Todd Duhnke Collection)

reduction gearboxes. The outer portion of the left wing and a piece of the left elevator was also nearby. Tree damage in the vicinity again showed that the fuselage fell in a near vertical descent.

The same techniques used in the still-unsolved Braniff crash were applied to this accident. Examination of the systems, engines and airframe revealed no operational failure or damage. A sustained, in-flight fire was ruled out. Although many witnesses saw the accident none could provide any useful clues. The weather, however, was one aspect of this accident that did not mirror the Braniff 542 crash. Although conditions were generally clear at the 18,000-foot cruising altitude, there were several reports of moderate-to-severe clear-air turbulence in the area.

Although the separation of the Northwest Electra's right wing appeared to be similar to the Braniff incident, investigation revealed the two were actually different. Reconstruction was conducted at the Lockheed factory in Burbank with particular attention given to the entire right wing and smaller portion of the left wing. Due to the parts distribution in the debris field, it was not possible to determine which broke off first. Both the front and rear spars of the right wing were fractured between the fuselage and the Number Three engine nacelle.

Both the upper and lower wing planks in the area of these breaks were shattered, leaving the adjacent material with a jagged edge. Laboratory investigation showed both compression and tension loads along this edge. Again it looked as if the wing had flapped. But this time movement was down as well as up. The CAB believed that as the wing motion began the planks shattered and the forward spar failed. With very little structural integrity remaining, the wing began to fold backwards, finally breaking the aft spar and falling away.

Inspection of the Number One engine indicated that a lower mounting assembly had failed with a clean tension break, allowing the power plant and propeller to oscillate up and to the left. This motion continued until the combination separated from the wing. The initial failure on the Number Four engine was an upper-left mounting at the firewall. The forward section of the engine and prop then moved down and to the right, rotating until it, too, separated from the airframe. Inside both the Number One and Number Four engines there was evidence that the compressor blades had rubbed on the inside of the compressor cases, further proving an abnormal rotation of the engine assemblies.

Again, the litany of possible causes for an in-flight breakup already rejected in the Braniff 542 were likewise dismissed in the Northwest 710 scrutiny. With a pair of seemingly similar and terrifying accidents just months apart, the Electra's integrity appeared questionable at best.

The hop from Minneapolis to Chicago was routine, and Flight 710 departed for Miami at 2:38 p.m. with six crew members and 57 passengers. It appeared to be proceeding as planned and communication with Air Traffic Control was normal until approximately 3:25 p.m. when the Electra broke up in flight six miles east of Cannelton, Indiana, near Tell City. All 63 aboard were lost.

The wreckage distribution pattern was strangely reminiscent of the Braniff 542 crash, with a debris field nearly seven miles long. It began with a few scattered parts and ended with a 40-foot crater containing the crushed fuselage. From this crater, back 11,291 feet along the axis of the debris field lay the right wing. Within 2,000 feet of the wing were the Number One and the Number Four engines, propellers and

Restrictions

A more detailed investigation of the 188 uncovered several cases of wing and propeller problems. After certification, Lockheed had continued testing its new airliner. During one dive test, the aircraft encountered turbulence while near its top design speed. Back on the ground a fuel leak led engineers to the discovery of damage under the right wing that was attributed to stress loads between the Number Three and Number Four engines. Electras already in service were reinforced between nacelles and the modification was made standard on the assembly line.

The Electra was originally certified with Aeroproducts propellers. During vibration surveys of the follow-on Hamilton Standards it was found that the outboard propellers were stressed to an unacceptable level, regardless of the propeller fitted. The cause was a torsional bending of the wing, corrected by tilting all four propellers upward three degrees. The fix also reduced vibration levels and noise within the cabin. Cost of retrofitting the existing fleet was born by Lockheed and ran in excess of $7 million.

Further difficulties were found as a result of forces encountered during landing. Cracks began to develop in the wing planks on both sides of the inboard nacelles. In the same area, fasteners that attached the planks to the wing ribs near the landing gear were coming loose. The fix consisted of fitting a doubler on the upper wing planks.

Finally, a fueling valve once stuck open and the wing structure was deformed due to over-pressurizing the tank. A service bulletin was issued reiterating proper fueling procedures.

Although annoying, these incidents did not indicate that there was anything fundamentally wrong with the Electra's structure. Any new type of airliner is expected to exhibit minor faults in need of rectification. During pre-certification trials the aircraft had performed without any major problems. Test flights were well in excess of anything that either the Braniff or the Northwest Electras would encounter on their fateful days. No one could figure out why the two aircraft came apart.

All of this notwithstanding, Federal Aviation Administration (FAA) head Elwood R. "Pete" Quesada issued an emergency airworthiness directive on March 20, 1960, reducing the Electra's 324-knot (370-mph) maximum cruise speed to 275-knots. Some observers questioned the validity of this move because both accident aircraft had been flying at less than the maximum cruise speed.

Two days later, representatives from Lockheed, Allison, NASA, the FAA, the CAB and the airlines held a closed-door meeting. The outcome was a multi-faceted approach to ensure that the 188 could stay in service, despite a call for grounding by several government and industry officials. A memo was issued on March 25, 1960, to all operators of the Electra. The maximum cruise speed was reduced again – to 225-knots – with a "never exceed" speed of 245 knots. Other actions included deactivation of the autopilot until this system was positively cleared as a possible factor in the accidents.

Also, several operational techniques were either modified or reemphasized, particularly with regard to pressure refueling. A comprehensive inspection of the wing, engines and nacelles, elevators and fuel tanks was to be completed within 30 days. The final result of this marathon series of meetings was for Quesada to call on Lockheed to conduct a complete engineering re-evaluation of the Electra. Assisting Lockheed in the task were Allison and NASA plus engineers from Boeing and Douglas. The pursuit of airline safety crosses corporate lines.

LEAP

One theory as to why the two Electras broke up was the phenomenon known, simply, as flutter. Present in all airplanes, flutter is the rapid, sometimes unnoticeable oscillation of a structure, such as a wing. It may be likened to the beating of a bee's wing. In an airplane flutter can be caused by many factors including excessive airspeed or entry into turbulence. Unchecked, flutter can destroy an airplane. Accordingly, engineers must design structures to dampen out this tendency. During several tests, the Electra proved to be highly flutter-resistant regardless of airspeed or turbulence. The question, then, was how and why two new airliners, flying at less than maximum design speed might have broken up due to flutter.

Lockheed instituted "LEAP" – Lockheed Electra Action Program – a comprehensive review of everything from design studies to flight-testing. The inquiry focused on stress and strength analysis, margins of safety, plus a re-examination of original Electra developmental data. In addition, the significance of damaged wing and nacelle components was explored to determine how it might affect aircraft integrity.

Wind tunnel testing was undertaken using three different models. The first was a nacelle-propeller unit examined at Lockheed's facility to assess stresses related to variations in pitch and yaw. Also checked at the same site was a one-eighth scale model of the Electra wing with two engines installed to allow measurement of nacelle and wing stiffness and loads with different fuel quantities. Finally, a one-eighth scale airframe at NASA's Langley wind tunnel was used to re-examine wing flutter characteristics. These were but a few of the many comprehensive wind tunnel tests and examinations conducted during LEAP.

The flight-test phase involved an Electra instrumented to record loads and stress in the wings, nacelles and engines. From gentle maneuvers with easy control inputs to extreme procedures with maximum control deflections, the 188 was put through its paces. Speed regimes varied from normal cruise to well past the design limit. Also explored was the flight control system along with the possibility that an autopilot malfunction might impart a sufficiently violent control force to separate a wing from the airplane.

In addition to engineering talent, Douglas loaned Lockheed a device designed to induce flutter oscillations in a wing. It consisted of a vane that was attached to the wingtip and moved to create the desired response. During more than 60 harrowing flights, test pilots tried

Electra from the Capital Airlines order undergoing LEAP modifications. (Todd Duhnke Collection)

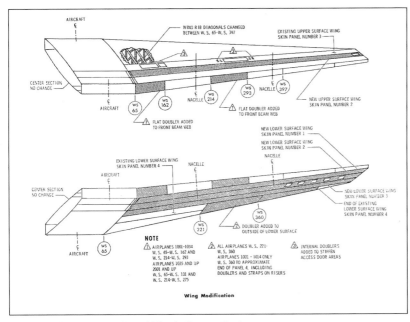

Wing modifications. (Lockheed Martin Corporation)

to pull the airplane apart. But the Electra continued to display a lack of susceptibility to uncontrolled, destructive flutter, even though two accidents appeared to be as a result of this phenomenon.

Flutter requires an external driving force, and since excessive airspeed and turbulence were ruled out, the quest was on to find what drove the wing to destruction. Even the clear-air turbulence encountered by Northwest 710, it was determined, would not have induced flutter. The phenomenon may have damaged the airframe but the forces normally found in turbulence are not of sufficient duration to sustain flutter.

Two other aircraft components can drive a wing to flutter; the control surfaces and the propellers. In this case, the control surfaces were discounted as not having enough energy to produce flutter. The propellers, actually large gyroscopes, had a stabilizing influence in regard to flutter. A spinning gyroscope tends to remain stable in its plane of rotation until some force acts upon it, at which time it will begin to wobble.

This effect, called "whirl mode," is present to some degree in all spinning objects and has been common knowledge for years. When applied to a propeller, whirl mode is counteracted by the rigidity of the engine/reduction gearbox mounting structure. The prop may wobble a bit but the magnitude of each cycle is reduced – or dampened – until the whirl mode ceases.

During thousands of flying hours the Electra's nacelles successfully dampened out whirl mode. However, wind tunnel testing showed that with a damaged or weakened mounting structure, whirl mode could actually increase in amplitude, further weakening the structure. This wobbling could continue to a point where it would impart oscillatory motion to the wing. The result was an induced, destructive flutter of the wing. This could happen well within the airplane's operating limitations. Evidence, often microscopic in scale, indicated that the nacelles that separated from the ill-fated Electras did experience the rapid reversals or wobbling associated with whirl mode.

On May 12, 1960, Lockheed President Bob Gross announced that both airliners broke up due to undampened propeller whirl mode that produced destructive flutter of the wing.

However, the question still remained: How did Braniff 542 and Northwest 710 suddenly succumb to its deadly effects? For whirl mode to increase unchecked there must have been a weakened component in the engine/propeller mounting structure. A search was undertaken to identify some incident in the short histories of these aircraft that could have

produced the required damage. In the case of Braniff 542 the only possible occurrence found was a poorly executed stall recovery during air crew training. The CAB surmised that the resulting recovery maneuver could have overstressed the aircraft even though the crew stated that their actions were not excessive.

Northwest 710 provided more telltale hints. The first was a reported hard landing when the flight arrived in Chicago. More likely was an encounter with clear-air turbulence that, although dismissed as causing the destructive flutter, may have weakened the mounting structure to the point where it could no longer dampen out whirl mode. The mystery remains to this day.

Belt and Suspenders

After determining that undampened whirl mode was the culprit, Lockheed moved LEAP to its next phase. Additional engine/reduction gearbox mounts were added to provide a more rigid structure and insure that, if any two mounts failed, the remaining three would suffice. One engineer likened the original mounts as a three-legged bar stool. If one of the legs breaks, the barstool and its patron will fall over. However, if two more legs are added to the same barstool, one could fail and it would remain stable; if two broke, the stool may tip a bit but will still remain upright.

The airframe structure to which the mounts were attached was also strengthened as were the surrounding nacelle panels. Even the air intake or "sugar scoop" attachment was modified. The wing itself was strengthened as well. Several wing planks, both top and bottom, were replaced with a heavier gauge material. Internally, numerous braces were added at key points and certain wing ribs were relocated and beefed up to help control stress. When complete, these modifications added more than 1,400 pounds to the Electra. Lockheed would pay for the fix – estimated to exceed $25 million – while individual airlines agreed to pay ferry costs to and from the Burbank plant.

With the accident causes and a fix in hand, Lockheed managers had to convince the government that the Electra was truly safe to fly. In June

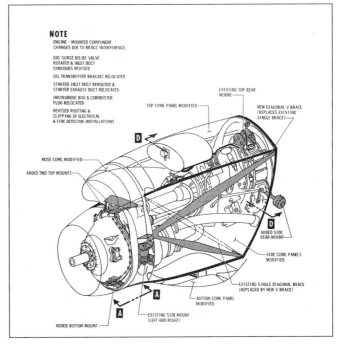

Engine-mounted component modifications.
(Lockheed Martin Corporation)

Back to Full Speed

A final flight test mandated by the FAA would nearly replicate the Braniff and Northwest accidents. The aircraft assigned – msn 1103 – was, ironically, being purchased by the FAA itself. For this investigation the nacelle structures had been deliberately weakened. Douglas flutter vanes were installed, and the Number Four drive shaft was disconnected and the propeller-blade-pitch locks disabled so the propeller would rotate uncontrollably.

In late December 1960, Lockheed test pilots Fish Salmon and Roy Wimmer departed from Burbank and pointed their Electra towards an area of known, constant turbulence. Completely confident in their aircraft, the pilots flew through turbulence at increasing airspeeds until well past those thought encountered by both the Braniff and Northwest Electras. The flutter vanes were activated and although the nacelles and wings were moving, the new structures controlled the motion and immediately dampened out the destructive flutter.

The airframe strained under this punishment but the whirl mode was under control. Over the next several days these flights were repeated again and again, each time validating the LEAP modifications. On January 5, 1961, the FAA announced that as each Electra was put through LEAP modifications, all restrictions would be lifted.

As 188s were scheduled to return from all over the world, Lockheed geared up for the rework program at Burbank that would involve a 22-day stay for each aircraft. Ansett's msn 1044 was the last to move down the LEAP assembly line, completing the project several months ahead of schedule.

Rebuilding Credibility

With the Electra given a clean bill of health, it was up to Lockheed and the airlines to convince a wary public that the airliner was safe to fly. The task was made more difficult by two more Electra crashes which occurred while the LEAP investigation was in progress; neither had anything to do with whirl mode or flutter.

Ansett-ANA Electra, the last of the LEAP 188s to be completed. It was returned to the airline on July 5, 1961. (Lockheed Martin Corporation)

1960, flight trials began anew with four modified aircraft. Test pilots sought the most turbulent air and exceeded every limitation, trying to rip the airliner apart.

Review of in-flight film footage would sometimes show nacelles and wings vibrating wildly, the wing planks undulating with waves as if they were made of some viscous liquid. In each case, the whirl mode and flutter were dampened out of existence. Ground-based engineers used racks to bend and twist the wing and nacelles well past the new design tolerances. As each modification passed muster, individual components were weakened and retested. For nearly six months the Electra endured this abuse, passing each test with flying colors. An engineer summed up LEAP as "belt and suspenders: If you want to fix the problem of your trousers falling down, you either wear a belt or suspenders. If you really want to be sure, you wear both."

Lockheed's people were sure they had fixed the Electra.

Braniff's N9706C (msn 1095) following LEAP, with the "Electra II" inscription on its tail. (Bryant Petitt Collection)

September 14, 1960; American Flight 361 (msn 1117 – N6127A)

The first accident occurred when another American Airlines aircraft crashed while landing at LaGuardia. *Flagship Phoenix* struck a runway dike and flipped over, but the fuselage stayed intact and there were no fatalities. The accident was blamed on pilot error, although the captain claimed he encountered a severe downdraft at the last moment. This type of accident could have happened to any airliner but since the Electra had been in the spotlight, the public ignored the demonstrated integrity of the fuselage and became more afraid of the airplane.

October 4, 1960; Eastern Flight 375 (msn 1062 – N5533)

Less than a month after the landing accident at LaGuardia Airport, another Electra went down, this time with more tragic results. Only 150 feet above the runway on takeoff from Boston's Logan Airport, the Eastern 188's left wing dropped, the nose pitched up and the airliner rolled over and into Winthrop Bay. Only 10 of the 72 passengers and crew survived. An investigation determined that on takeoff, the aircraft had flown through a large flock of starling birds, sustaining numerous strikes; in addition, the engines ingested several carcasses. At the point where the Electra flew through the flock, there were more than 100 bird carcasses on the runway.

The Number One engine had automatically shut down and its propeller feathered. The Number Two and Four power plants both experienced large fluctuations in power output that caused the aircraft to yaw wildly as the airspeed rapidly decreased. The Number Three engine, operating at full power, contributed to the loss of control.

Although the pitot tubes were never recovered, they could have been blocked by bird ingestion thus giving erroneous airspeed information to the flight crew. The windscreens may also have become obscured as a result of bird strikes. As late as 1962, the FAA released a report stating that the Electra produced a noise that sounded like the chirp of a cricket and may have actually attracted the starlings.

Although the CAB attributed the crash to bird ingestion and resultant loss of control, an alternate theory was put forth by a National Airlines pilot. The scenario centered around the first officer's seat, which had been written up for a faulty fore-and-aft locking mechanism and was apparently improperly repaired. When the Electra hit the birds and violently yawed due to power fluctuations, the first officer would have to put in nearly full right rudder. This might have caused the seat lock to fail, sliding the seat aft. The first officer would then have pulled back on the yoke as he slid back, thus pitching the nose of the aircraft up and precipitating the stall. The theory is plausible, but since none of the crew survived the accident, it could not be proven.

Rebuilding Confidence

In the wake of five crashes, Lockheed and airlines managers did not sit idly by and hope the tragedies would fade from memory. On the contrary, they started an aggressive campaign to soothe the flying public's fear of the airliner. Leading the campaign was American Airlines. With the cooperation of the other Electra operators, AA managers initiated what were known as "fact teams" or "truth squads."

Beginning in November 1960, even prior to LEAP, these pilots, engineers and public relations staffers traveled from city to city giving briefings to civic leaders and politicians. Rather than try to hide the truth, the teams openly explained whirl mode and flutter, the investigation and the re-engineering effort. American also conducted a series of inexpensive excursion flights.

Several airlines renamed the aircraft in an effort to portray a new and improved airliner. Monikers like "Electra II" and "Super Electra" were painted on the sides of LEAPed 188s. Najeeb Halaby, the new head of the FAA and a former test pilot, put the airliner through its paces, then stated, "I would not hesitate to have my family travel in Electras."

As load factors began to climb, it appeared that the dark days were finally over. The Electra went on to provide excellent service for both its original buyers and its subsequent operators. Over the next 37 years there were more accidents but none were so totally without explanation as Braniff 542 and Northwest 710.

A memorial at the accident site of Northwest Flight 710. (Phil Brooks)

Chapter IV
SUBSEQUENT OPERATORS

Holiday Airlines' N971HA (msn 1091) displays the airline's first colors in September 1972 while pausing at Lake Tahoe, California. (Robert D. Archer)

As mentioned earlier, several original operators began to phase out the Electra when the design was less than a decade old. With the advent of the Boeing 727 and Douglas DC-9, many 188s were soon up for sale. Considered by many to be a still capable airliner, few sat unused for any length of time.

The Cargo Modification

Lockheed produced all 170 of its Electras as pure-passenger airliners. However, with an increasing number of used airframes available, carriers began to look at the 188 as a viable freighter. Responding to this marketing opportunity, Lockheed Aircraft Service Company (LAS) of Ontario, California, designed an appropriate cargo conversion. The modification took several forms based on customer options and was priced between $350,000 and $500,000 per aircraft in 1968 dollars.

Northwest N136US undergoing cargo modification at Lockheed Aircraft Service Company, Ontario, California. (Todd Duhnke Collection)

Two types of main flooring were offered, one heavy-duty for bulk cargo and one lighter weight for palletized loads. Operators could also choose a single cargo door forward of the wing or specify an additional door aft, both upward opening, sliding inside the fuselage.

Finally, several "combi" models were produced which allowed a configuration for both passengers and freight, separated by a movable fuselage bulkhead. The modified airframes began rolling off the line in 1968 and when complete, received a new model designation. The 188A became the 188AF; likewise the C became the CF, while combi models, regardless of original designation, became PFs.

In addition to LAS, other firms completed cargo modifications for the Electra. Among these was American Jet Industries (AJI) of Van Nuys, California, which took over the program started by defunct California

Lockheed modifications offered the option of one or two cargo doors. (Lockheed Martin Corporation)

Model 188CF of Channel Express showing the outward opening American Jet Industries cargo door. (Channel Express)

More unusual were the bulk-fuel tankers completed by R. E. Dolan of Anaheim, California, for use on the Alaskan North Slope. This highly specialized modification involved installation of a beefed-up deck that accommodated 18 interconnected tanks, a fueling/defueling pump and a control panel in the cockpit. Two aircraft (msns 1059 and 1064) were so fitted.

A number of Miami companies also did work on Electra freighters. Batchair, Inc., and ESCO Service Company altered a handful of 188s for light freight work by fitting a strengthened deck and tie-downs; however, no cargo doors were installed. The Addison Company developed a modification that consisted of an aft cargo door and a fuselage cargo handling system which was installed in several 188s. Another Miami firm involved was General Air Service, a repair station that was contracted to install the Addison modification.

Secondary Operators

Many company managers welcomed second-hand Electras into their fleets, in passenger, freight and combi configurations. In fact, several operators flew the type longer in continuous service than the airlines that originally bought factory-delivered 188s.

The following operators are listed in alphabetical order except when grouped under one parent company or adjusted for aesthetic reasons.

Airmotive Corporation. AJI undertook several conversions that included stronger flooring, a pallet loading system and one or two outward and upward opening cargo doors. Amazingly, these 90-day cargo conversions were still being undertaken to aircraft originally built more than 18 years earlier, confirming the type's value as a reliable and economical freighter able to operate from 5,500-foot runways.

HK-775 in Aerocondor's first Electra livery. (Airliners Collection)

AEROCONDOR	
msn	*Registration*
1063	HK-1416
1073	HK-775
1077	HK-1845
1081	HK-1415
1083	HK-774
1087	HK-1976
1115	HK-777

Aerocondor, S.A.

Aerovias Condor de Colombia was flying a mixed fleet of Douglas DC-4s, DC-6s and Curtiss C-46 Commandos when, in April 1969, the company purchased its first 188A from American Airlines. By January 1971, five ex-Flagships had been delivered and Electra service began the following May 1, between Colombia and Miami, Florida.

Two freighters were added in the mid-1970s, both of which had been owned by several different carriers. Aerocondor lost one passenger Electra in August 1973 and a freighter in 1975. Two 188As were sold to VARIG, one each in November and December 1975. Aerocondor ceased operations in late 1978; the remaining two passenger Electras and sole freighter were put in storage at Barranquilla, Colombia.

An ex-American Airlines 188A, HK-774 was purchased by Aerocondor in 1969. (Harry Sievers Collection)

Seen at Miami, Aerocondor's 188CF HK-1845 reflects a white crown skin livery. (Terry Waddington Collection)

Seen at Miami in October 1975 is this Aerocosta Colombia 188CF (msn 1077). *El Caribe* was soon re-registered HK-1809 although the company sold it to Aerocondor less than six months later. (Bruce Drum)

Aeroservicios de California bought msn 1036 in late 1972 and flew it within Mexico for just over six years in passenger service. (Ted Gibson)

Aerovias was formed at Guatemala City in 1986. This 188CF (msn 2022) was added to the fleet in 1991. It was sold less than one year later. (via Eddy Gual)

Air Andes International of Ecuador leased this 188A (msn 1031) for five months in 1975. Although not yet converted to a cargo configuration, the aircraft appears to be hauling freight as evidenced by nets visible in the aft windows. (Bruce Drum)

Ready for delivery to Air Bridge, msn 1036 still wears a U.S. registration in this July 1992 photo. (via Eddy Gual)

Air Bridge Carriers
Hunting Cargo Airlines

Air Bridge Carriers (ABC) was founded in November 1972 as a cargo-only airline in Great Britain. Operating out of a base at East Midlands, the company has flown a variety of freighters including the Vickers Vanguard Merchantman, the Armstrong Whitworth Argosy and the Handley Page Herald. The first Electra was leased from an American company in late 1988 and over the next several years numerous 188s were flown for varying periods of time.

The Hunting Group has owned Air Bridge since its inception and, during a 1992 reorganization, changing ABC's name to Hunting Cargo Airlines. There was no real difference in the operation other than the name and aircraft livery. The company began flying UPS overnight freight services linking Shannon and Dublin with Cologne starting in September 1992. Other runs included Aldergrove–Coventry–Brussels–Vienna–Athens.

A year later, the Hunting Group founded an additional air cargo division in Ireland called Hunting Cargo Airlines (Ireland) Ltd., based at Dublin. Both divisions flew the Electra, some of which were owned outright while others were leased for a time and later returned. Also, several airframes went back and forth between the two divisions and have worn different registrations while with the same company.

In mid-1998, the remaining Electras were withdrawn from service and stored. Two were acquired by Channel Express for parts and broken up at East Midlands. Atlantic Airlines bought one for parts, plus a pair to be placed in service following heavy maintenance.

AIR BRIDGE/HUNTING CARGO	
msn	Registration
1036	G-FNWY
1039	N355WS
1112	N360WS
1116	N669F
1129	EI-HCE
1131	N667F
1138	EI-HCF
1144	EI-CET
2003	EI-CHW
2006	EI-CHX
2014	EI-CHY
2015	EI-CHZ

Hunting Cargo Airlines began flying 188CF G-FIZU (msn 2014) in 1993, on freight runs throughout Europe. It was re-registered EI-CHY in 1997. (via Eddy Gual)

A Former Northwest 188C, N123US (msn 1082) was leased by Air California for Lake Tahoe service. It is seen at New York-LaGuardia in 1973. (Airliners Collection)

Air California

Founded in 1966 as an intrastate carrier, Air California began with a fleet of four Electras – two ex-American and two ex-QANTAS. Service commenced on January 16, 1967, between Santa Ana's Orange County Airport and San Francisco. Two Douglas DC-9s joined the fleet prior to the end of 1967.

By the close of its first year in business, Air California had carried more than 300,000 passengers. Actively looking for equipment to replace both the 188s and the DC-9s, the airline selected Boeing's 737. In late 1968 the Electra fleet was sold to an aircraft leasing company, then leased back by Air California and flown until March 1969.

In July 1970 the carrier purchased a single 188C (msn 1082) and operated it for the San Diego Padres baseball team and on other charter flights. By the mid-1970s, Air California was preparing to serve Lake Tahoe and, like its competitor PSA, was forced by local noise restrictions to fly quieter turboprops. Thus, in February 1975, the carrier restarted Electra airline service with three aircraft. When Lake Tahoe operations were suspended in late 1979, Air California's remaining 188s were sold to Mandala Airlines.

AIR CALIFORNIA	
msn	Registration
1006	N125AC
1050	N278AC
1082	N123AC
1100	N289AC
1114	N124AC
2002	N359AC
2004	N385AC

Re-registered N123AC, msn 1082 appears in an updated livery at San Francisco International in September 1978. The Electra spent more than eight years with Air California. (Nigel Chalcraft)

Originally with Eastern Air Lines, Air Florida's N64405 (msn 1075) in original colors at Miami in September 1973. (Bruce Drum)

Air Florida

Another intrastate carrier initially, Air Florida commenced operations in September 1972 with a single Boeing 707-321. Serving only three cities from the start, it was clearly evident to the airline's management that a replacement for the gas-guzzling jet was in order. In March 1973, the Boeing was replaced by two leased 188Cs; a third was obtained in August 1974; all were eventually purchased outright.

Despite the fielding of more economical airliners and an expanding route structure, the 1970s were tough on Air Florida. The company found

that competing against giant Eastern Air Lines – plus National and Southern – was not an easy proposition, even with the addition of a leased Boeing 727 in 1976.

When Ed Acker joined the Air Florida as CEO the following year, one of his goals was to use the investment money he had raised for a fleet upgrade. Five ex-Air Canada DC-9-15s were purchased along with options for more, thus numbering the Electras' days. The first was sold in March 1977 and the final two in July and August of the same year. All went to an aircraft leasing company.

AIR FLORIDA	
msn	Registration
1075	N23AF
1111	N25AF
1144	N24AF

N138US, photographed at Miami in 1974 with larger titles, later became N24AF. (Bruce Drum)

N23AF is seen at Miami in 1976 with smaller fuselage titles. (Todd Duhnke)

Delivered to KLM in December 1959, PH-LLD (msn 2009) was leased to Air Ceylon in January 1960 for one year. Converted to a 188CF in 1969, this aircraft crash-landed in 1985 while with Galaxy Airlines. (Terry Waddington Collection)

Miss Voyager is the title given to Air Manila International's PI-C1063 (msn 1096), which was leased between 1973 and 1978. The carrier flew three other Electras (msns 1007, 1008 and 1021), including two lost in accidents. (Airliners Collection)

Leased off and on throughout the early 1990s, ALM Antillean Airlines 188AF N665F (msn 1100) is seen taxiing at Miami in October 1991. It is currently in Great Britain with Atlantic Airways. (David G. Powers)

Founded in 1995 by Heinz Amerer, the Austria-based airline that bears his name is amassing a small fleet of Electras. Included is ex-Ansett 188AF N356Q (msn 1039) which was acquired in December 1996. (Airliners Collection)

Honduras-based Electra Freighter of ANSHA Cargo (msn 1060) was originally operated by Eastern Air Lines. Prior to joining ANSHA, it was converted to a 188AF. (Terry Waddington Collection)

After conversion to 188CF standards, this ex-Eastern Air Lines aircraft (msn 1098) was leased by Barbados-based Carib West Airways. The Electra was returned from lease in 1978; Carib West went out of business in 1980. (Terry Waddington Collection)

From the defunct Capital order, then repossessed from Sports Aloft, N182H finally began service with American Flyers Airline in January 1963. (Terry Waddington)

American Flyers Airline (AFA)

American Flyers operated as a non-scheduled, passenger charter airline specializing in U.S. Military contracts. In need of an aircraft with sufficient range and payload to be profitable both domestically, across the Atlantic and to Hawaii, AFA began phasing out its aging Constellations and DC-3s in favor of the Lockheed Electra. The first two were nearly new Model 188Cs (msns 1135 and 1136) that were purchased in January and February 1963.

Part of the Capital Airlines order, these two aircraft were originally delivered to Sports Aloft, Inc. After this firm was unable to commence operations, the Electras were finally bought by American Flyers. In April 1966, the company lost one aircraft (msn 1136) when it crashed on approach to the airline's home base airport at Ardmore, Oklahoma, killing all aboard including AFA founder Reed Pigman (see Chapter Six).

Beginning in June 1966, four ex-Northwest 188Cs were purchased, bringing the fleet up to five. AFA's Electras were configured to be self-sufficient with a turbine-powered Auxiliary Power Unit (APU) in the tail to provide air for engine starts. A cockpit temporary navigator station, designed to fulfill overseas flight requirements, was utilized as required.

By 1968, expenditures were exceeding revenues and talks of a merger

AMERICAN FLYERS	
msn	Registration
1077	N122US
1085	N124US
1101	N125US
1105	N126US
1135	N182H
1136	N183H

began between American Flyers and Universal Airlines, another Electra operator. In January 1970, a single 188 (msn 1007) was sold to Holiday Airlines. When Universal bought American Flyers in June 1971, the remaining four Electras, considered redundant by the new owners, were eventually sold to an aircraft leasing company.

Atlantic Airlines

Atlantic Airlines can trace its lineage back to 1969 when General Aviation Service, Ltd. began air-taxi operations. The ensuing years saw the company grow and field several corporate titles and divisions including Air Atlantique, Atlantic Air Transport and Atlantic Airways. All catered to specific markets with either passenger or freight service.

In 1993 the first Electra began operations and soon after Atlantic Cargo, Ltd. was formed. Overnight mail contracts were undertaken, plus small package services on behalf of such customers as DHL, TNT and UPS. By early 1998, a fleet of five 188 freighters had been assembled for overnight freight contracts and other charters throughout Europe. Two more Electras were acquired later in the year from Hunting Cargo, plus a third to be parted out. The Atlantic Cargo name was changed to Atlantic Airlines in March 1998.

ATLANTIC AIRLINES	
msn	Registration
1100	G-LOFC
1129	G-FIJV
1131	G-LOFB
1138	G-FIJR
1143	G-LOFD
1144	EI-CET
2002	G-LOFA
2014	G-FIJU

Seen in Great Britain in June 1998, G-LOFD sports Atlantic's latest livery. (Peter J. Clukey)

VR-HFO, one of two former Lockheed Electra prototypes flown by Cathay Pacific. Both airframes were scrapped in Ecuador in 1981. (Lockheed Martin Corporation)

Cathay Pacific Airways

In one sense, Hong Kong-based Cathay Pacific Airways could be considered an "original" operator since it purchased directly from Lockheed and none of the aircraft had seen prior commercial service. The airline actually placed an order prior to the first flight of the Electra. If considered a secondary operator of the type then, the airline was the first to fly a used 188.

In any case, Cathay Pacific received two 188As in June and April 1959. Lockheed, having used the aircraft in the test and certification program, then completed conversions to Cathay Pacific's specifications. Interestingly, there is some information that indicates these two airframes were originally intended for Aeronaves de Mexico; however, details are sparse and no sale was completed.

Cathay Pacific used its pair of Electras to service Far Eastern routes, many of which had been inherited when the firm took over local rival Hong Kong Airways in 1959. The 188s flew alongside company DC-3s, -4s, and -6s, to destinations including Manila, Taipei, Tokyo, Bangkok and Singapore as well as points in Australia.

By 1962 the DC-3s were gone and the first Convair 880 introduced. The following year all the Douglas airliners were retired and the two 188s and single Convair jet comprised Cathay's entire fleet. With the purchase of an additional 880 in 1965, one Electra (msn 1004) was sold, followed by the second two years later as Cathay standardized on pure jets.

CATHAY PACIFIC	
msn	Registration
1002	VR-HFN
1004	VR-HFO

VR-HFN appears in the later and more familiar Cathay livery. (ATP/Airliners America)

Originally with Northwest, msn 1112 was converted to a 188CF in 1985 and passed through several owners before being leased to Charrak Air, an Australian cargo company. The Electra freighter was based at Cairns, North Queensland, and used for shipments of tuna to Japan starting on April 23, 1996. It was returned the following January, ending Charrak's Electra service. (Peter J. Gates)

Shown in a later livery, N360Q was leased from May 1997; photographed in April 1998. (Terry Waddington Collection)

Channel Express Air Services, Ltd.

Express Air Services was founded in 1978 as a passenger and cargo charter carrier operating out of the Bournemouth-Hurn Airport in Great Britain. Renamed Channel Express Air Services in 1984, the firm flew an assortment of mid-sized airliners including Handley Page Heralds and de Havilland DHC-6 Twin Otters.

The first Electra, a 188CF (msn 1075) leased from Zantop, arrived in December 1989. The ensuing years saw Channel Express operate several different Electra freighters and, by 1998, the fleet had stabilized at five, with three owned outright. In addition the company has increased its fleet size via leases from others, including Falcon Cargo and Zantop, for use on contract flights for United Parcel Service (UPS) and the UK's Royal Mail Skynet system.

At press time, a Lynden Air Cargo Electra freighter was acquired on a 12-month lease.

CHANNEL EXPRESS	
msn	Registration
1035	N341HA
1038	N344HA
1053	N343HA
1068	G-CHNX
1075	G-OFRT
1091	G-CEXS
1104	N284F
1107	N285F
1112	N360Q
2003	EI-CHW
2015	EI-CHZ

COPA Panama entered the turbine age in 1971 with the acquisition of a single Electra. Two more, including this ex-Eastern 188C (msn 1071, for a time registered HP-654) joined COPA in 1974. All were withdrawn by the early 1980s. (Terry Waddington Collection)

The second Electra prototype was bought by Ecuatoriana in 1967, following service with Cathay Pacific. Never converted to freighter configuration, it migrated to TAME and was scrapped in 1981. (Bruce Drum)

Compania Ecuatoriana de Aviacion, S.A. – Ecuatoriana

Transportes Aereos Militares Ecuatorianos – TAME

Originally formed in 1957, Ecuadorian flag carrier Ecuatoriana began acquiring Electras in 1967, initially with a single aircraft, and gradually increased the fleet during the next few years for use on domestic and international routes. One Electra (msn 1087) was leased for just two months at the end of 1972.

Two 188s were disposed of prior to the suspension of Ecuatoriana operations in July 1974. Its Electras were taken oven by TAME, a transport division of the Ecuadorian Air Force, and placed into domestic service a few days later with both civilian and military registrations.

TAME lost a pair of Electras in accidents, but continued to operate the remaining four into the 1980s. Two were withdrawn and broken up, while the last two went on to other operators.

	ECUATORIANA/TAME
msn	Civilian/Military Registration
1002	HC-AMS/FAE-1002
004	HC-ANQ/FAE-1004
1031	HC-AYL
1040	HC-AZT/FAE-1040
1042	HC-AQF
1050	HC-AZL/FAE-1050
1052	HC-AZY/FAE-1052
1087	N7138C
2002	HX-AVX
12004	HC-AZJ/FAE-2004

The dual registration on the vertical stabilizer of this 188A indicates that it was operated both by civil airline TAME and the Ecuadorian military. Shown at Quito, it wears an attractive two-tone blue livery. (Ueli Klee)

Operated for passenger charter, ex-Western 188A N7136C was sold to the Argentine Navy in 1983. (Jon Proctor Collection)

Evergreen International Airlines

When Evergreen Helicopters bought the operating certificate of defunct Johnson International Airlines in November 1975, a new subsidiary was formed, called Evergreen International Airlines. As such, the firm offered a wide variety of services, including support for fighting forest fires plus non-scheduled passenger and cargo flights.

The Johnson International purchase included three Electras and, over the next 15 years, Evergreen would buy, operate and sell a total of eight different airframes. Some were configured and operated as passenger airliners and later converted for cargo, while others were freighters when acquired. One was sold to Air California in March 1977 while another migrated to Galaxy International Airlines in 1981. In 1983 a single Electra was parted out at Marana, Arizona, the same year in which a batch of three 188s was sold to the Argentine Navy.

Evergreen also actively leased portions of its Electra fleet to various airlines around the world before finally selling the last two (msns 1068 and 1091) in late 1990.

EVERGREEN	
msn	Registration
1006	N1006T
1068	N5535
1070	N5536
1072	N5534
1074	N5558
1091	N5539
1121	N5532
1123	N5538

Evergreen purchased msn 1091 in 1979 and converted it to a 188CF. It was sold to Channel Express 1990. (Jon Proctor Collection)

N402FA (msn 1085) was originally with Northwest. Converted to a 188CF in 1975, it was leased by Fairbanks Air the same year, for North Slope oil operations in Alaska. The airframe currently sits in the fire pit at Greenville, South Carolina. (John B. Hayes)

The Fairbanks Air lineage is obvious, being renamed in mid-1975, as seen on this 188PF, one of four operated by Great Northern Airlines. N405GN (msn 1094) was eventually broken up. (Jon Proctor Collection)

Fiesta Air N300FA (msn 1077, shown) along with N301FA (msn 1020) were operated by Fiesta Air, a small charter carrier based at Long Beach, California, and owned by the Hawthorne Christian College. Electra operations began in the fall of 1971 and continued until the company declared bankruptcy in April 1973. (Harry Sievers Collection)

Falconair's SE-FGB (msn 1098), the first of three 188Cs operated by the carrier for less than two years. (Terry Waddington)

Falconair Charter AB

Falconair began commercial charter operations from its Malmo base in May 1967 with three Vickers Viscount 784D turboprops. The airline's first Electra (SE-FGB) was received in December 1968. A second (SE-FGA) arrived the following month, with SE-FGC added in December 1969; all were C models originally with Eastern Air Lines and acquired on lease.

In addition to shorter flights, the Electras flew to popular vacation destinations including ski charters to Geneva and Salzburg, plus warm weather vacation trips to the Mediterranean.

Following a change in ownership, Falconair suffered a downturn in business and ceased all flying on September 1, 1970. Two Electras were returned to the leasing company while the third was sold to Sterling Sweden AB.

FALCONAIR	
msn	Registration
1075	SE-FGC
1088	SE-FGA
1098	SE-FGB

Purchased in 1986, this 188CF (SE-IVT, msn 2015) served Falcon Cargo for about five years and was chartered extensively by Channel Express. (Terry Waddington)

FALCON CARGO	
msn	Registration
2003	SE-IVS
2006	SE-IVR
2014	SE-IZU
2015	SE-IVT

Falcon Aviation AB

Founded in 1965 as a chartered passenger and freight airline, Malmo, Sweden-based Falcon Cargo flew mostly light aircraft. Two decades later the fleet expanded to include Electra Freighters; three 188CFs entered service in late 1986, with a fourth added in October 1987. The name Falcon Aviation was adopted in 1992 and, a year later, all four Electras were operated on behalf of Hunting Cargo Airlines.

Two of the Electras were broken up while a third was sold to Channel Express; msn 2006 is now stored at East Midlands.

Fleming International Airways
Cam Air International
Spirit of America Airlines

Established in 1973, Fleming International was a Miami, Florida-based all-cargo operator, specializing in both scheduled express freight and subcontract work. Starting with a single cargo version in 1974, the carrier would, over the next decade, operate 10 Electras, obtained from a variety of sources. One was lost in a 1977 accident at St. Louis.

Fleming International went out of business in 1983 only to be reincarnated the same year under the name Cam Air International and continue the former company's 188 cargo operations. Due to declining revenues, Cam Air was also forced to close its doors barely a year later.

A merger in 1986 with Spirit of America Airlines saw the entire fleet of Electras under new ownership. It was almost inevitable that Spirit of America would cease operations, which it did in 1989. The aircraft were all sold to different parties.

FLEMING/CAM AIR/ SPIRIT OF AMERICA	
msn	Registration
1066	N664F
1076	N280F
1085	N402GN
1092	N666F
1094	N405GN
1096	N4465F
1100	N665F
1116	N669F
1131	N667F
1144	N668F

N280F was converted to 188AF specifications in 1968 and leased to Fleming International from 1974. It crashed on takeoff from St. Louis, Missouri, on July 6, 1977. (Bruce Drum)

N669F in full Cam Air colors at San Francisco in 1985. (John Kitchen)

Shown in all-white with red titles, Spirit of America's N402GA after acquisition from Great Northern. It is now stored. (Keith Armes)

Belgian-owned, Zaire-based FilAir was established in 1992 and acquired four former VARIG Electras in the mid-1990s for operations in Africa. In addition to msn 1040 (shown), 9Q-CXU (msn 1041), 9Q-CUU (msn 1137) and 9Q-CVK (msn 1139) were also procured. Only 9Q-CXU remains active, in a combi configuration. (via Eddy Gual)

Fred Olsens Flyselskap A/S

In aviation since 1933, Oslo, Norway-based Fred Olsens acquired three Electra freighters in 1973 to replace piston equipment. Nearly two decades later, three additional units were added. In addition to on-demand cargo charters, the carrier operated extensive services on behalf of DHL, and applied that company's markings to its aircraft.

Fred Olsens' aviation division ceased operations at the end of April 1997; LN-FOG was sold to Atlantic Airlines in June 1997, with LN-FOH leased to Amerer Air from March 1998.

The four remaining Electras were moved to Coventry in December 1997 and remain stored at that location. LN-FON, -FOL and -FOO retained DHL colors, while LN-FOI 12/29 still wears the full company livery.

FRED OLSENS	
msn	Registration
1098	LN-FOO
1116	LN-FOL
1128	LN-FON
1143	LN-FOG
1145	LN-FOH
2005	LN-FOI

Fred Olsens operated a number of Electra freighters including 188CF, LN-FOI, seen at Oslo, Norway. (Terry Waddington)

Originally flown by American Airlines, this 188 was converted to an Electra Freighter in 1977 and has been operated by several companies. Fred Olsens purchased the aircraft in 1991 and flew it of behalf of DHL. (via Eddy Gual)

Galaxy's livery reflects the colors of COPA - Panama, the source of its first two Electras, including N5532 (msn 1121) which was lost in a 1985 accident. (Peter Rentzsch)

Galaxy Airlines

Based at Fort Lauderdale, Florida, Galaxy began Electra charter flights in 1983 with two 188s acquired from COPA - Panama. Both passenger and cargo operations were carried out during the next few years, utilizing additional 188s leased from Evergreen and Transamerica. Closely following the loss of N5532 in January 1985, N854U was forced to crash-land with a landing gear problem.

Although Galaxy continued in business, the accidents caused temporary suspensions of service and government scrutiny that ultimately resulted in cessation of operations in mid-1988.

GALAXY	
msn	*Registration*
1068	N5535
1071	N511PS
1091	N5539
1121	N5532
1147	N188LC
2009	N854U
2020	N511PS

Another of the defunct Capital Airlines fleet, msn 1135 appears in the livery of charter operator Gulf Air Transport, which operated it in a passenger configuration during the early 1980s. The 188C was sold in 1985 and converted to freighter configuration the same year. It was scrapped at Opa-locka in 1996. (Charles E. Stewart; Harry Sievers Collection)

Guyana Airways leased Electra freighter 8R-GEW (msn 1035) in 1976 and flew it for less than one year from its Georgetown hub. Two other Electras (msns 1105 and 1109) were also acquired for short-term leases a year earlier. (Bruce Drum)

Hawaiian's N5525 (msn 1038), seen prior to being re-registered N344HA. (Bill Curry)

Hawaiian Airlines

From 1978, Hawaiian operated its Mainland Air Cargo Division from a base at Macon, Georgia, under the Hawaiian Air Cargo banner. Ten Electra freighters were planned for this service and military charter work, with the first arriving in February. The endeavor was short-lived, however, and discontinued in September of the same year after only eight 188s had been received. The operation was later taken over by Zantop, along with the fleet.

HAWAIIAN AIR CARGO	
msn	Registration
1035	N341HA
1038	N344HA
1043	N346HA
1053	N343HA
1075	N347HA
1098	N345HA
1109	N340HA
1128	N342HA

Holiday Airlines

Originally a de Havilland Dove operator, Holiday acquired two Electras – including the first prototype – in 1968 for service between Oakland, San Jose and Burbank, California, and Tahoe Valley Airport at Lake Tahoe, California. Los Angeles and San Diego received service later and a third Electra joined the fleet in mid-1974, not long before the under-capitalized company closed its doors in February 1975.

HOLIDAY AIRLINES	
msn	Registration
1001	N974HA
1091	N971HA
1114	N972HA

Holiday's N972HA, seen in April 1975 wearing a later color scheme (Harry Sievers Collection)

Internacional de Aviacion of Panama acquired HP-684 (msn 1128) in September 1977 and flew it for less than a year. (Harry Sievers Collection)

Perth, Australia-based Indian Ocean Airlines acquired this former Eastern 188A (msn 1036) on lease in 1992. Registered VH-IOB, it was to operate passenger flights to Cocos and Christmas Islands. Unfortunately, bureaucratic delays forced the carrier into liquidation before 188 service could begin. The aircraft rests following its return to Opa-locka, Florida, in January 1993. (Airliners Collection)

The only Electra registered in Iceland, TF-ISC (msn 1096) was obtained by Iscargo Iceland in late 1979 following cargo conversion. It later flew with Eagle Air as TF-VLN. (Harry Sievers Collection)

IJA's CF-IJY wears the name *Yukon Lady* in this photo taken at Calgary in October 1973. (Brian Blatherwick; Henry Tenby Collection)

International Jet Air

Established in late 1969, IJA began operating a single Electra on inclusive-tour flights and gained the distinction of flying the first Canadian-registered 188; both passenger and combi variants were utilized. The company set up initial Electra operations for Panarctic Oil and Dome Petroleum, ferrying crews to Arctic drilling sites and, at times, landing on gravel or ice surfaces.

IJA also operated CF-IJR (msn 1127) for Imperial Oil. Charter flights carried entertainers on tour, gamblers en route to and from Nevada, and professional athletic teams. A total of 10 Electras flew for IJR before the last three were sold to NWT Airways in 1975 when the company ceased operations.

INTERNATIONAL JET AIR, LTD.	
MSN	*Registration*
1094	CF-IJY
1108	CF-IJM
1127	CF-ZSR
1128	CF-ZST
1129	CF-IJV
1131	CF-IJW
1138	CF-IJR
1141	CF-PAB
1143	CF-IJC
1145	CF-IJJ

International Jet Air operated CF-IJR for Imperial Oil, in support of that company's Norman Wells refining operation, plus its Beaufort Sea exploration project. The 188PF is seen at Edmonton International in June 1975. (Brian Blatherwick; Henry Tenby Collection)

Intermountain Aviation bought 188A N1006T (msn 1006) in 1972, primarily for government contract charter work. A second Electra (msn 2004) was leased as well. The owned aircraft was sold in 1975; Intermountain was bought by Evergreen later that year. (Ted Gibson)

N7136C (msn 1074), leased by Johnson Air in 1972, was one of three Electras (including msns 1006 and 1070) operated chiefly on U.S. Forest Service contract flights. Like Intermountain, the company was bought in 1975 by Evergreen International, which took the Electras as part of the deal. (Larry Smalley; Henry Tenby Collection)

LAB-Lloyd Aereo Boliviano bought 188A CP-853 (msn 1125) from American Airlines in 1968. Sold five years later to the Bolivian Air Force, it was reported to be in storage at La Paz. (Terry Waddington Collection)

LACSA of Costa Rica operated two Electra freighters. TI-LRO (msn 1088) a CF model, was leased from July 1977 until 1981. Msn 1109 was acquired in 1976 but sold off two years later. (Bruce Drum)

"Super Electra C" ZP-CBX served LAP just short of 20 years. It is one of three Electras bought from Eastern, having originally worn registration N5521. (Terry Waddington Collection)

LAP – Lineas Aereas Paraguayas

LAP purchased three Electras from Eastern Air Lines in December 1968 to replace its fleet of Convair 240s on routes connecting Paraguay with neighboring countries. The first 188 entered service three months later, flying from Asuncion to Buenos Aires, Argentina; Sao Paulo and Rio de Janeiro, Brazil; and Montevideo, Uruguay. Later, service began to Salta, Resistencia and Jujuy in Argentina, and Lima, Peru. Santiago flights began several years later.

Until Boeing 707s were acquired, Electras were utilized for VIP presidential flights to both the United States and Europe. The Boeings, which first arrived in 1978, were used for new overseas flights and did not begin taking over Electra routes until the mid-1980s. Two 188s were then placed in open storage while the third (ZP-CBZ) remained airworthy for use when needed; it was sold in 1994. The remaining pair was to join new Paraguayan carrier Zoma Airlines in 1994; however, the company was not able to commence operations and the Electras remain stored at Asuncion.

LAP	
msn	*Registration*
1032	ZP-CBX
1078	ZP-CBY
1080	ZP-CBZ

A VARIG Electra taxies past as LAP's ZP-CBZ starts engines at Sao Paulo's Congonhas Airport on December 23, 1984, prior to departure on its regular service to Asuncion. (Stefano Pagiola)

Lynden Air Cargo's Electra freighter N285F, photographed in August 1996. (Henry Tenby)

Lynden Air Cargo

A family of several transportation and logistics companies, Lynden, Inc. serves the northwestern United States and Alaska with connections worldwide. Beginning in 1954 with ground freight service along the Alaskan Highway, the company has grown into more than a dozen subsidiary companies. Of these is Lynden Air Cargo, which was founded in 1995 and operates a cargo-only service out of Anchorage.

To fly Alaskan by-pass (Special 4th Class) mail for U.S. Postal Service, Lynden amassed a fleet of three Electra freighters leased from Zantop. The 188s operated alongside the company's three Lockheed Hercules freighters; a fourth 188 was acquired in 1996, with ad-hoc charter work undertaken; all four aircraft were eventually purchased outright.

In mid-1998, it was announced that Lynden planned to dispose of the Electras and standardize around its "Herk" fleet, although the 188s were still in use at press time. One (msn 1107) was leased for a year to Channel Express.

LYNDEN AIR CARGO	
msn	*Registration*
1079	N281F
1107	N285F
1110	N289F
1148	N287F

N287F is seen at Lynden's Anchorage base in 1996. Originally leased from Zantop, the aircraft was subsequently purchased outright. (via Eddy Gual)

LANSA – Lineas Aereas Nacionales, S.A.

Intent on increasing capacity for a growing tourist trade, LANSA began acquiring a small fleet of 188s in 1969. All were purchased from Boeing, having been accepted as trade-ins from Braniff. Based in Lima, Peru, and flying mainly to high-altitude airports, the Electra's exceptional performance in these conditions was welcomed by the airline and its flight crews.

LANSA's first aircraft – msn 1106 – arrived in August 1969, only to crash less than a year later. Two more were brought on line in August and October 1970, followed by another in April 1971. When a second accident claimed msn 1086 on Christmas Eve 1971, the Peruvian government revoked LANSA's operating certificate and the two remaining Electras were grounded.

LANSA	
msn	Registration
1086	OB-R-941
1095	OB-R-945
1106	OB-R-939
1114	OB-R-946

Photographed in September 1970 at Opa-locka, this freshly painted LANSA Electra is most likely OB-R-941, which crashed on Christmas Eve 1971. (Harry Sievers Collection)

Mandala Airlines

Founded in 1969, Mandala Airlines of Indonesia was one of the last havens for prop-driven airliners, flying a variety of types well beyond their disappearance from many of the world's air routes.

The airline acquired six Electras between the end of 1979 and mid-1983 for use on domestic routes. Except for the loss of msn 2008 in 1985, the turboprops served Mandala well. Three were withdrawn in 1989 while the remaining two soldiered on until near the end of 1994, replaced by jet equipment. All were eventually acquired by Air Spray of Canada.

MANDALA		
msn	Registration	Name
1006	PK-RLF	Rengga Gading
1026	PK-RLH	Giung Wanara
1082	PK-RLD	Dick Pitaloka, Kencana Wungu
1114	PK-RLE	Rengganis
2008	PK-RLG	Jaya Perkasa
2020	PK-RLI	Aryo Bantati

PK-RLF was originally the engine development aircraft used by Allison. After a number of operators, it was purchased in 1980 by Mandala. (Terry Waddington Collection)

N6106A in April 1969 with Lake Havasu City titles. (Harry Sievers Collection)

McCulloch International Airlines

McCulloch Properties formed a Long Beach, California-based air charter division in mid-1969 for the purpose of transporting potential customers to its various land development sites in Arizona, Nevada, Colorado and Arkansas. Acquiring the operating certificate of defunct Vance International Airlines at the end of 1971, the parent corporation formed McCulloch International Airlines a few months later, transferring its seven Electras to the new company. Four more were acquired (and another was leased briefly) for the operation that also included contract work with NASA and the U.S. Navy, athletic charters and other specialized flying.

Fleet size was dictated by available business, and some of the 188s served McCulloch for a year or less. Four Boeing 720Bs were added in 1975, cutting the Electra count to four by 1976. The carrier ceased operations in 1979.

McCulloch	
msn	Registration
1028	N6106A
1051	N6112A
1056	N6114A
1058	N6115A
1072	N6118A
1075	N23AF
1102	N6124A
1116	N6126A
1120	N6129A
1121	N6130A
1122	N6131A
1123	N6132A

McCulloch's N6118A reflects the immaculate condition which was a hallmark of this operator. (Harry Sievers Collection)

Seen wearing full McCulloch colors in March 1976 at Omaha, Nebraska, N6106A was chartered to carry Elvis Presley's entourage during a concert tour. The entertainer's Convair 880 *Lisa Marie* is in the background. (Todd Duhnke)

Seen outside a VARIG maintenance hangar is msn 1126 in the colors of New Air Charter Service, a Zairian airline based at Kinshasa. This 188A was written off in 1994; three others migrated to Trans Service Airlift after New Aces suspended operations in 1996.
(Gianfranco Beting)

Delivered to Western Air Lines in 1961, msn 1143 was converted for that company to a 188AF in 1969. Nordic Air of Sweden bought the aircraft in 1972, along with msn 1145 (LN-MOI) and sold both to Fred Olsens only 15 months later. (Airliners Collection)

NWT Air's C-FNWY receives service on a clear winter day in 1988 at YZF. (NWT Air)

NWT Air – Northwest Territorial Airways, Ltd.

Founded by Bob Engles as a Canadian bush operator at Yellowknife in 1961, NWT Air grew from float planes to larger piston-powered aircraft before starting Electra service between Calgary and Edmonton in late 1976. CF-IJV (msn 1129) was acquired from International Jet Air, along with a large spares inventory.

A proven performer in the rugged Northwest Territory of Canada, the Electra performed a variety of passenger and passenger-freighter roles, and was joined by three more 188s by 1984. One of the more exotic routes performed was a combi service on the trans-NWT route between Yellowknife, Rankin Inlet and Frobisher Bay. The company also acquired

NWT Air	
msn	*Registration*
1036	CF-NWY
1129	CF-IJV
1138	CF-IJR
2010	C-GNWC
2015	C-GNWC

Electras on short-term leases as needed. NWT Air began using the type for a nightly transcontinental "Gold Label" courier service in 1983, from Vancouver to Calgary, Edmonton, Winnipeg and Toronto. Operating on behalf of Air Canada; this arrangement continued until 1987, the year NWT Air became an Air Canada Connector.

Barely 12 months after founder Engles retired in 1990, NWT Air – by then wholly owned by Air Canada – withdrew the Electras. The airplanes, each originally bought by NWT Air for between $250,000 and $350,000 were sold for approximately $2 million and $2.5 million apiece (Canadian dollars).

Passengers disembark from Electra Combi C-FIJV, shown with earlier Northwest Territorial titles. (NWT Air)

N178RV in modified colors while on lease from Reeve Aleutian. (Trevor Ogle; Henry Tenby Collection)

Although its lineage dates back to 1946, the first operations under the Nordair name began in 1957 with DC-4 equipment on a Montreal–Frobisher Bay route with en route stops. In addition to a pair of Electras acquired for government ice patrol work (see page 106), the airline purchased 188CF CF-NAX (msn 2010) in 1972. Netting visible in the passenger windows indicates cargo usage. The airplane was withdrawn and stored in 1976. (PFI-Plane Fotos International; Harry Sievers Collection)

CF-PAK (msn 1127); one of two Combi Electras operated by Panarctic Oils, Ltd. to oil sites in northern Canada. Sister ship CF-PAB (msn 1141) was lost in a 1974 accident. (Brian Blatherwick; Henry Tenby Collection)

On final approach, ONA's *Ranger,* N284F. (Terry Waddington)

Overseas National Airways (ONA)

Specializing in both passenger and cargo charters, New York-based ONA began its association with the Electra in January 1968 and by April the fleet numbered eight ex-National aircraft. Lockheed Air Services at Ontario, California, converted all these airliners to freighters and ONA used them to supplement its existing stable of DC-8s and DC-9s.

The company twice leased a single passenger 188 (msn 1032 in 1968 and msn 1135 in 1971) to complete specific charters, operating each for less that one year. Overseas National's traditional business, however, was the Military Airlift Command's cargo charters. An increase in demand prompted the purchase of two additional Electra freighters in mid-1972.

A final airframe (msn 1058) was obtained in September 1973, primarily for parts, and was subsequently scrapped. Later, a downturn in business and a so-called "fleet realignment" saw the 10 remaining Electras sold in 1974; most went to Zantop.

ONA	
msn	*Registration*
1032	N5521
1058	N6115A
1076	N280F
1079	N281F
1084	N282F
1089	N283F
1104	N284F
1107	N285F
1110	N289F
1133	N290F
1135	N182H
1146	N286F
1148	N287F

N182H, seen at Miami in 1971. One of two passenger Electras flown by ONA, it passed through several operators before being broken up in 1996. (Bruce Drum)

CF-PWG, photographed in May 1973. (Brian Blatherwick; Henry Tenby Collection)

Pacific Western Airlines

PWA leased two second-hand Electras (msns 1127 and 1128) in 1971 for scheduled services and charter work. A year later, the second pair were acquired on lease for flights between Calgary and the Beaufort Sea. Replaced by jet equipment, the last Electra left in April 1976.

Passengers and freight board simultaneously on Combi CF-ZSR, leased by Pacific Western for 19 months in 1971-72. (PWA)

PWA	
msn	*Registration*
1035	CF-PWG
1064	CF-PWQ
1127	CF-ZSR
1128	CF-ZST

N356Q (msn) 1039 was converted by Ansett Airlines, its original operator, to a 188AF in 1972. After several owners it is now with a Florida leasing company, which provided the aircraft for one year to Renown Aviation in the mid-1990s. Renown currently flies a passenger Electra (N351Q; msn 1036) on contract with the U.S. Navy, between the North Island NAS and the California Channel Islands. It is also used for other contract work. The airline has two additional Electra freighters (N360Q; msn 1112 and N285F; msn 1107) wet-leased to Channel Express. (Jon Proctor Collection)

N9744C on a cold day in Alaska. LAS converted it to a 188PF in 1968. (Gianfranco Beting)

Reeve Aleutian Airways (RAA)

Based in Anchorage, RAA was incorporated in March 1947 by Robert C. Reeve, a veteran aviator who had been flying in Alaska since the early 1930s. Reeve and his airline specialized in flying from Anchorage to remote airports along the Aleutian Island chain. During the 1960s, military charter flights were undertaken, and a route to Seattle (later withdrawn) was awarded in 1979.

In the late-1960s, the Lockheed Electra was selected to supplement (and later replace) Reeve's DC-6s. A 188C (msn 2007) was purchased from Air New Zealand in February 1968. Service began in June over the Anchorage–Cold Bay–Adak route. Although this aircraft was never modified as a PF Combi, it can be configured to haul both passengers and light freight such as mail, which is loaded through the forward passenger door.

Two 188PF Combi models – msns 1140 and 1118 were bought from Western Airlines in 1970 and 1972, respectively, fitted with 28 passenger seats aft. Unfortunately, msn 1118 succumbed to a hangar fire in November 1974.

Three years later, Reeve Aleutian leased and subsequently purchased a 188A (msn 1038) for use on a contract awarded to fly Trans-Alaska pipeline personnel from Anchorage to points north. The aircraft was

En route from New Zealand to Alaska in 1968, N1968R appears on the ramp at its Burbank birthplace, resplendent in Reeve colors.
(Terry Waddington)

traded in March 1978 to American Jet Industries for a 188PF (msn 2010) which was deemed more appropriate for the airlines' usual operations. Finally, a single Electra (msn 1046) was purchased from Zantop in September 1983. After filling in during the extensive repairs on msn 2007 (see Chapter Six), it saw limited service before being parked and gradually broken up for spares.

In 1995, Reeve replaced Markair on the Anchorage-to-Bethel, Alaska, route with the Electra taking over for Markair's pure-jet equipment. Despite flying in some of the worst weather and into rather primitive airports, safe and routine Electra operations have been the norm at Reeve. Msns 1140, 2007 and 2010 – dubbed "Super Aleutian Electras" – came to represent the world's last front-line airline 188 passenger operations.

Sadly for Electra aficionados, the airline announced in September 1998 that it would retire its three 188s by March 31, 1999. The economic reality of increased maintenance costs caught up with an aircraft type that has been the mainstay of Reeve Aleutian for 30 years.

Aboard N178RV, somewhere between Anchorage and Bethel. (Henry Tenby)

RAA	
msn	*Registration*
1038	N5525
1046	N7135C
1118	N7140C
1140	N9744C
2007	N1968R
2010	N178RV

N178RV, originally with TEAL, was purchased by Reeve in 1978. (via Eddy Gual)

Royal Air Lao christened ex-Trans Australia Airlines 188A XW-PKA (msn 1061) *Tiao Anou*. The company leased the passenger Electra (along with msn 1069) in May 1972, and operated it for one year. This airframe was scrapped in 1976. (Terry Waddington Collection)

SAHSA of Honduras purchased 188A HR-SHN (msn 1060) from Eastern in 1969 and had it converted to a freighter eight years later. The aircraft retains a basic TAN livery in this 1992 photo, following return from lease to that carrier. SAHSA also flew msn 1018 as HR-SAW. (via Eddy Gual)

SAM Colombia
Sociedad Aeronautica de Medellin Consolidada

Reorganized in 1962, SAM Colombia operated a fleet of DC-4s on domestic services and routes to Central America, along with a cargo operation to Miami. The carrier began acquiring Electras from Eastern Air Lines in 1969 and flew eight of the type until all were repossessed by Eastern in February and March 1977.

SAM		
msn	Registration	Name
1005	HK-554	Mercurio
1010	HK-1274	Venus
1013	HK-553	Jupiter
1014	HK-557	Marte
1029	HK-555	Neptuno
1030	HK-1275	Pluton
1043	HK-691	Apollo
1053	HK-692	Saturno

SAM Colombia 188A HK-555 reveals cargo netting in the windows, indicating cargo use. (Bruce Drum)

Southeast Airlines leased passenger 188C N23AF (msn 1075) in 1977 for just one year. The carrier ceased scheduled flying in late 1979. (Bruce Drum)

One of only a few Electras to appear on the French registry is F-OGST (msn 2002). Converted to a 188CF in 1976, it was leased in 1987 by Servicios de Transportes Aereos Fueginos, a cargo firm based at Buenos Aires, Argentina and operated for five years. The aircraft was christened *Lago Fagnano.* (Keith Armes Collection)

With roots as a travel agency in Denmark, Sterling Airways began tour operations in 1962 with a DC-6B. In 1970 this 188C (msn 1075) was purchased from Falconair and operated by Sterling's Swedish subsidiary. It was sold in 1973. (Bo-Goran Lundkvist)

N859U (msn 2016), originally named *Ceres* with KLM. (Airliners Collection)

Universal Airlines

When Universal Consolidated Industries bought Zantop Air Transport in September 1966, it formed a subsidiary company called Universal Airlines, which continued Zantop Air's primary business of air shipping auto parts out of Detroit. Flying an assorted fleet of Douglas propliners and Curtiss C-46s, the company began purchasing 188s in March 1968.

By early 1969 Universal had a fleet of 13 Electras acquired from KLM and PSA. Lockheed Aircraft Service Company subsequently completed freighter conversions on all the airframes.

Two of the ex-KLM aircraft were lost in accidents in August 1970 and March 1972. Mishaps notwithstanding, financial problems forced Universal into bankruptcy in May 1972, and the remaining 11 Electras were immediately repossessed. The ex-KLM 188s went to Saturn Airways while the two ex-PSA aircraft were acquired by Overseas National Airways.

UNIVERSAL	
msn	*Registration*
1110	N862U
1133	N863U
2001	N851U
2003	N852U
2006	N853U
2009	N854U
2012	N855U
2013	N856U
2014	N857U
2015	N858U
2016	N859U
2017	N860U
2018	N861U

Saturn Airways
Trans International Airlines
Transamerica Airlines

When Universal Airlines ceased operations in May 1972, the U.S. Air Force and its Military Airlift Command (MAC) were placed in an awkward position. There was still a requirement to conduct several regular cargo missions but no airline to fly them. Oakland, California-based supplemental carrier Saturn Airways stepped in and picked up the contracts, only to find itself suddenly short of capacity. To solve this problem, the company leased the nine ex-Universal Electras freighters from the finance companies that had repossessed the aircraft. Saturn resumed the MAC flights less than one week after Universal had shut down and in June 1974, purchased the 188 fleet outright.

Around the same time the company began negotiations with Trans-International Airlines, also Oakland-based, for a possible merger. The deal was finalized in December 1976 with Trans-International taking over Saturn and the nine 188 freighters. In October 1979, the company was renamed Transamerica Airlines, after its parent company Transamerica Corporation.

Over the ensuing years Transamerica would experience periods of boom and bust. In the early 1980s most of the Electras were was placed in

The lineage of N861U (msn 2018), shown in three different liveries (above and opposite page). The Saturn scheme is a holdover from Universal Airlines. (Bruce Drum)

(Terry Waddington Collection)

(via Eddy Gual)

storage at Marana, Arizona, with some occasionally pulled out and leased to other operators. The sell-off began June 1983 with single airframes disposed of from time to time until the firm finally ceased operations in September 1986. The last Electra was sold in March 1987.

With one final breath, Transamerica Corporation restarted Trans-International Airlines in April 1987 utilizing a single leased Electra and two DC-8s. Barely surviving one year, this company shut its doors in June 1988.

SATURN/TIA/TRANSAMERICA	
msn	*Registration*
2003	N852U
2006	N853U
2009	N854U
2013	N856U
2014	N857U
2015	N858U
2016	N859U
2017	N860U
2018	N861U

Trans International's first livery, retained with new Transamerica titles on 188CF N854U (msn 2009). (via Eddy Gual)

TACA International Airlines of El Salvador bought two Electra freighters in 1976, replacing a single DC-6B on runs to Mexico, the U.S. and other Central American cities. In addition to YS-06C (msn 1147, shown) TACA operated YS-07C (msn 1069). Both were withdrawn by the mid-1980s. (Terry Waddington Collection)

HR-TNN (msn 1067) of Honduran airline TAN (Transportes Aereos Nacionales, S.A.), which owned and operated the 188A between 1970 and 1982, appears in initial and updated colors. The carrier also flew HR-SAV and -TNL (msns 1060 and 1134).

Transafrik operated S9-NAF (msn 2022) in Africa between 1987 and 1991. The final Electra built, this 188CF was sold to Aerovias Guatemala in 1991. S9-NAH (msn 1056) also flew for Transafrik. (Eddy Gual)

Freight operator TPI International bought 188C N360Q (msn 1112) in 1985 and had it converted to freighter configuration. It was repossessed in 1992. (Pete Crawford; Phil Brooks Collection)

Msn 1048 is seen wearing both the U.S. registration of its former owner, Eastern Air Lines, and the Zairian registration of TRAMACO, which purchased the 188AF in 1987. (Gianfranco Beting)

Transcarga leased N107DH (msn 2013) in July 1992 and operated freight services in Europe on behalf of Iberia. (Bob Shane)

Originally *Flagship Baltimore* with American Airlines, PP-VJW (msn 1124) poses for the camera in 1978. (Henry Tenby)

VARIG – Viacao Aerea Rio-Grandense, S.A.

VARIG's long and fruitful association with the Electra actually began as a result of negotiations started by a different Brazilian airline. REAL – Redes Estaduais Aereas, Ltda. – approached American Airlines in 1961 with an offer to purchase a number of redundant 188s. However, before the sale could take place, VARIG bought out REAL and, although not bound by any former contracts, accepted the Electra deal anyway. Between August and October 1962, five ex-American 188s flew south to Brazil to begin domestic service in September 1962.

VARIG had commenced pure-jet flights prior to the REAL acquisition, starting with the Caravelle in 1959 and the 707 in 1960. However, so favorably did the company view the Electra that, unlike its North American counterparts, it actually replaced jet aircraft (Caravelles) with turboprops. The French jet was gone by 1964 as the 188 took over more and more premier domestic sections. Favoring the Electra was the fact that jet aircraft were prohibited at that time from operating out of Santos Dumont Airport, located only minutes from downtown Rio de Janeiro. Also, the multiple short legs that characterized VARIG's domestic route structure were better

suited to the Electra. Between November 1967 and April 1970, four more ex-American aircraft joined the fleet, followed in June by two ex-Northwest 188PFs for cargo flights. In February 1970, msn 1049 was damaged beyond repair at Porto Alegre Airport.

One exceedingly successful Brazilian airline program in which VARIG Electras participated was the *Ponte Aerea* or "Air Bridge," equivalent to the Eastern Air Shuttle, although VARIG's version predated it. Of all the routes in Brazil, none is so dense with passenger traffic as the run from Rio de Janeiro to Sao Paulo. Operating from Santo Dumont and Congonhas Airports, respectively, both are only minutes from downtown business centers; the segment was a natural for the Air Bridge.

VARIG and two other airlines – Cruzeiro do Sul and VASP – formed a pool agreement to serve this route starting in July 1959, with all companies

VARIG	
msn	*Registration*
1024	PP-VJL
1025	PP-VJM
1037	PP-VLN
1040	PP-VNK
1041	PP-VJO
1049	PP-VJP
1050	PP-VNJ
1063	PP-VLX
1073	PP-VLY
1093	PP-VLC
1119	PP-VJU
1123	PP-VJW
1126	PP-VJV
1137	PP-VLB
1139	PP-VLA

A busy morning at Congonhas Airport in November 1991 includes four Electras on the flight line. With a population of more than 17 million, Sao Paulo is the world's third-largest city. (Gianfranco Beting)

The slow retirement of VARIG's Electra fleet began in December 1991, in favor of Boeing 737-300 equipment. Still resisting the new generation, PP-VNJ (msn 1050) rests at the end of another long day. It was among the last Electras to join VARIG's fleet. (Gianfranco Beting)

flying similar piston aircraft. The mid-1960s saw a rapid increase in passenger boardings and the Electra joined *Ponte Aerea* on an irregular basis in the colors of both VARIG and VASP (Viacao Aerea Sao Paulo).

Following a rash of accidents, the government banned the use of two-engine aircraft on the Air Bridge in March 1975. Eight VARIG Electras, having been replaced on other routes by Boeing 737-200s, were assigned exclusively to *Ponte Aerea*. The airline even converted its two cargo-carrying 188PF turboprops back to passenger configurations for Air Bridge flying. Some of VARIG's Electra flights were operated (still in full company colors) on behalf of VASP and Transbrasil as part of the pool contract.

In late 1976, VARIG purchased a pair of ex-Aerocondor 188s to help

overcome a capacity shortage as Electras became the exclusive equipment on *Ponte Aerea*. Two more were purchased in April 1986 from TAME Ecuador.

Always heavily involved in the control of the *Ponte Aerea*, the Brazilian Government decided In the early 1990s that the Electra should be replaced by more modern equipment. After more than 30 years of service with VARIG, the 188 phase-out began in November 1992 and was completed by January 1994. As a tribute to the faithful turboprops, one airframe – msn 1025 – was donated to a museum at Rio de Janeiro, where it resides today in full VARIG colors.

Charter operator Winner Airlines purchased msn 1018 from Eastern in April 1970. Registered B-3057, it was returned only two months later and may not have flown any revenue flights for the Taiwan-based company. The Electra is shown at Oakland, California, en route back to Miami from the Far East. (Larry Smalley; Henry Tenby Collection)

Seen at Willow Run Airport in 1983, N364HA is a 188AF, with non-Lockheed cargo doors. (via Nicky Scherrer; Jon Proctor Collection)

Zantop International Airlines

As mentioned earlier, Zantop Air Transport operated as Universal Airlines until May 1972 when it went out of business.

Zantop reestablished itself in May 1972 by taking up the remains of Universal and forming Zantop International Airlines. Working closely with the automotive industry, the airline became an Electra operator in 1974 when it purchased nine aircraft from Overseas National. Six more arrived during 1977–78, bought from Eastern. In 1980 an additional seven freighter versions were obtained from Hawaiian Airlines' defunct Mainland Air Cargo Division. The airline bought other aircraft from time to time and would eventually fly 25 different Electra freighters. It also occasionally leased 188s to cargo airlines both in the United States and abroad.

By the mid-1990s, Zantop's fleet had been reduced through aircraft sales, scrapping and accidents. In 1997, the operation was scaled back considerably. Both the fleet and the company are presently for sale, and most of the Electras remain stored at the airline's Detroit-Willow Run headquarters.

ZANTOP			
msn	*Registration*	*msn*	*Registration*
1009	N5504	1079	N281F
1012	N5507	1084	N282F
1014	N5510L	1089	N283F
1017	N5512	1098	N345HA
1022	N5516	1104	N284F
1023	N5517	1107	N285F
1033	N5522	1109	N340HA
1034	N5523	1110	N289F
1035	N341HA	1128	N342HA
1038	N344HA	1133	N290F
1043	N346HA	1146	N286F
1046	N7135C	1148	N287F
1053	N343HA		

N7135C was one of two operated by Trans Continental Air Transport. Zantop purchased it in 1978 and apparently flew the Electra without a formal cargo conversion. Sold to Reeve Aleutian in 1983, it only operated for a few months before being reduced for spare parts and then broken up. (Harry Sievers Collection)

N282F was modified by Lockheed in 1968 and purchased by Zantop four years later. It was photographed in March 1979 with a bare metal livery. (Terry Waddington Collection)

Chapter V

NON-AIRLINE OPERATORS

N927NA, the third Electra prototype, was converted to an NP-3A test-bed and later acquired by NASA. (Harry Sievers Collection)

The Electra has proven adaptable to missions that were never envisioned when it was designed. From early on the military was actively courted and would eventually fly hundreds of what were basically modified 188s. Governments and private companies also found the aircraft suitable for their specific applications. From research aircraft to private transports and fire bombers, variations of this venerable aircraft have only been limited by the operators' imagination.

The Military

Many concepts that made up the Electra came from the C-130 Hercules military transport design. Indeed, some original Lockheed studies show an

aircraft remarkably similar to the "Herk" (see page 9). Eyed as a potentially lucrative customer, the military was presented with ideas including transports for personnel, litter patients and cargo. Also presented – in concept only – were aircraft for navigator training and electronic warfare operators. None of these proposals came to fruition.

Although the logical military Electra would have been a transport aircraft, the hands-down winner in Lockheed's search for a non-airline customer was the United States Navy and its P-3 Orion. The Navy wanted a replacement for the more than 12-year-old Lockheed P2V Neptune that would continue the role of a land-based Anti-Submarine Warfare (ASW) aircraft. In addition to seeking significant improvements in performance, the Navy wanted an "off-the-shelf" platform with an already proven design.

Lockheed was awarded a contract in April 1958 for a stock Electra conversion to provide the test aircraft. Initial modifications to msn 1003 consisted of fairings for a semi-external weapons bay just ahead of the wing and a Magnetic Anomaly Detector (MAD) "stinger" on the tail. The first test flight on August 19, 1958, was used to evaluate aerodynamic changes. After this assessment, the fuselage was shortened by seven feet and mission-related electronic gear installed; it received the designation

Artist's view of a proposed U.S. Air Force transport. (Lockheed Martin Corporation)

Early impression of the P-3 Orion. (Lockheed Martin Corporation)

P-3B Orion – BuNo 151383 – of Patrol Squadron VP-64, Willow Grove, Pennsylvania. (T. L. Brown)

YP3V-1 (Bureau Number 148279). So modified, the aircraft flew for the first time on November 25, 1959. The Navy liked what it saw and placed an order for the first P3V Orion. Over the years hundreds would be produced. (The 1962 transition of all U.S. military aircraft designations changed P3V to P-3.)

The P-3A model had stronger wings than the Electra and held more fuel. It was equipped with water-methanol injected, 4,585 eshp Allison T-56 engines. An internal weapons bay was located forward of the wings; all up, the P-3A weighed 11,500 pounds more than its civilian counterpart.

The upgraded P-3B – first delivered in February 1966 – consisted mainly of ASW sensors and weapons equipment plus the addition of uprated T-56 engines that just nudged 5,000 eshp. The P-3C first flew in September 1968. It varied from the B primarily with regard to the electronic gear installed; the model has been continuously updated to this day. Current studies speculate that there will be no replacement for the P-3C before 2016.

In addition to the ASW Orion, several specialized versions have emerged for a variety of uses including staff transport, electronic eavesdropping and weather tracking. More than 600 P-3s have been produced, including foreign military sales and license-built Orions.

RP-3A of VXN-8 – BuNo 158227 – used to map the earth's magnetic field. (InterAir)

P-3A of the Naval Research Laboratory. (InterAir)

A Norwegian P-3B. (Candid-Aero Files)

Not an Orion, Argentina's aircraft are former Electras. This aircraft – 6-P-103 – is msn 1070. (via Eddy Gual)

Also with the Argentine Navy, 5-T-2 (msn 1120) started out as N6129A with American Airlines. (Harry Sievers Collection)

Aero Union operates a growing fleet of ex-Navy Orions as fire bombers. (via Eddy Gual)

Air Spray Long Liner C-FQYB – msn 1063. (Airliners Collection)

Fire Bombers

Both the Electra and the Orion have been employed in the role of airborne fire suppression units. More than fire bombers, the aircraft are actually faster and more accurate retardant delivery systems, allowing more time on the fire than their aging non-turbine counterparts.

Aero Union of Chico, California, began by fitting a 3,000-gallon retardant tank to ex-Navy P-3As in 1990. It now has seven of the type in its fleet and is adding one new aircraft per year on average.

In 1994, Air Spray of Edmonton, Alberta, Canada, began assembling a fleet of "Air Spray Long Liner" Electras. In cooperation with Aero Union, these aircraft were fitted with what has been titled the "Constant/Variable Flow Tank System." This drop system is controlled by an on-board computer that allows for precision placement of the load.

Another Canadian operator, Conair of Abbotsford, British Columbia, obtained a single 188 (msn 1060) and attached the same 3,000-gallon tank normally fitted to its DC-6s. Company managers state that this is just an interim conversion as they plan a fleet re-equip with the C-130. The DC-6 tank did not penetrate the floor of the aircraft so Conair is able to use this Electra as a freighter in the off-season.

Conair's sole Electra fire bomber C-FZCS (msn 1060). (Conair)

C-FQYB dispenses a load of fire retardant. (Air Spray)

Federal Aviation Administration (FAA)

In February 1961, the FAA purchased a single 188C (msn 1103) originally ordered by the Hughes Tool Company but not taken up. Based in Oklahoma City, Oklahoma, this Electra was initially used for flight training. In 1972 it was modified for work as a flight check aircraft to inspect airways and navigational aids. Turned over to the General Services Administration in 1977 for disposal, it was transferred to NASA in September 1978.

Former FAA N111 – msn 1103. (Lockheed Martin Corporation)

Still with the FAA in 1975, msn 1103 was photographed at Honolulu, wearing an updated livery and re-registered N97.
(Harry Sievers Collection)

Re-assigned N428NA looks smart in updated NASA colors. (NASA)

National Aeronautics and Space Administration (NASA)

NASA has operated the Electra and P-3 mainly out of its facility at Wallops Island, Virginia. In 1967, the agency received a NP-3A, N428NA, which was built as the third Lockheed Electra prototype (msn 1003) before being modified as a test-bed for the P-3 program.

N428NA (originally NASA 427, then N427NA) operated from the Johnson Space Center in Texas as part of the Earth Survey Fleet until 1977 when it was transferred to Wallops Island. Finally, in 1993, this aircraft was donated to the National Museum of Naval Aviation in Pensacola, Florida, for static display.

The original FAA Electra was registered N429NA and flown from the Wallops facility. This aircraft was disposed of in 1997 and broken up for spares. A final P-3B was brought on line in the early 1990s; registered N926NA, it is still in use today.

This fleet of Lockheed products has seen a varied employment by NASA. Over the years it has been fitted with imaging radar, surveillance radar, remote sensing equipment, lasers, lidar (similar to radar but used to replace radio waves with light waves) and other geo-science features.

The second NASA Electra – 188C N429NA – seen in April 1988. It was later scrapped. (via Eddy Gual)

NASA's current P-3B – N926NA. (NASA)

Travel Clubs

Several second-hand Electras were picked up by individuals and leasing companies for use as private passenger transports. One popular operator type was the travel club, an organization in which the club members embarked on vacations aboard their "own" airliner. Some 13 different travel clubs flew the Electra, although in a few cases, for short periods of time.

TRAVEL CLUBS					
Organization	*msn*	*registration*	*Organization*	*msn*	*registration*
Adventures Travel Club	1031	N5017K	Holiday Wings	1109	N172PS
Aeroclub International	1105	N126US	Jet Set Travel Club	1131	N131US
Aeronauts International	1144	N138US	Nomads	2008	N836E
Air Holiday	1020	N301FA	Ports of Call	1135	N8355C
	1075	N64405	Shillelaghs of Washington	1101	N125US
	1111	N128US	Vagabond Air Travel Club	1085	N124US
Century 2000	1096	N5009K	Voyager 1000	1088	N11VG
	1105	N126US		1096	N5009K
FPE Travel Club	1144	N138US		1098	N12VG

Adventure Travel Club's 188C (msn 1031) at Fort Lauderdale in 1972. (Bruce Drum)

N126US (msn 1105) of Aeroclub International at Miami in 1971. (Bruce Drum)

Aeronauts International little changed the Northwest livery on its 188C N138US (msn 1144). (via Eddy Gual)

Only the name has changed. Century 2000's 188C, still wearing former Aeroclub livery in this 1973 photo taken at Miami. (Bruce Drum)

Originally with QANTAS, Detroit-based Nomads flew 188C N836E (msn 2008). (Terry Waddington)

Denver Ports of Call's immaculate 188C N8355C (msn 1135). (Harry Sievers Collection)

Out of the U.S. Capital, Shillelaghs operated 188C N125US (msn 1101). (Bruce Drum)

Vagabond Air Travel Club operated ex-Northwest 188C N124US (msn 1085) on lease for 18 months. (Bruce Drum)

The Los Angeles Dodgers baseball club operated this 188A N1R (msn 1006), seen at Los Angeles in 1969. (Ted Gibson)

American Airlines' N6128A (msn 1119) flew charters for U.S. Vice Presidential candidate Hubert H. Humphrey in 1964. (Larry Smalley; Henry Tenby Collection)

Based at Indianapolis, Indiana, Voyager 1000 Travel Club N11VG (msn 1088) – *Miss Indianapolis* – along with N12VG (msn 1098), flew members in the early 1970s. (Bruce Drum)

United States Customs Service

In the early 1980s Lockheed saw an opportunity to compete with Boeings E-3 Sentry in the Airborne Early Warning and Control (AEW & C) arena with a less expensive, modified Orion. A former Australian P-3B was fitted with a rotodome and first flew on June 14, 1984.

The plan was to either modify a customer's P-3 or if desired, build new AEW & C airframes to order. By the close of 1986 no customers had stepped forward for either proposal.

Despite a lack of enthusiasm by military for the AEW & C aircraft, the U.S. Customs Service embraced the design and began flying the type in May 1989. A fleet of four rotodome-equipped and four stock P-3s has been assembled and operates from the Naval Air Station at Corpus Christi, Texas. These aircraft patrol the U.S. southern border and also deploy detachments to other countries.

On the ramp at NAS Corpus Christi in July 1997, a "slick" (above) and a "dome" (below) await the next U.S. Customs mission. (David G. Powers)

A former PSA 188C, NCAR has been flying N308D since 1975. (NCAR)

National Center for Atmospheric Research (NCAR)

In May 1973, NCAR leased a former PSA Model 188C (msn 1130). By December 1975 the organization purchased the Electra and registered it as N308D. Based in Boulder, Colorado, the airplane is currently used for a variety of atmospheric experiments and has been modified to carry such equipment as Doppler radar, radiometers and a vacuum system for collecting air samples. Numerous ports and hard points have been installed for the mounting of temporary sensors.

N308D, bristling with collection devices. (C.T. Robbins)

NOAA's two WP-3Ds were custom built for their present use. (NOAA)

National Oceanic and Atmospheric Administration (NOAA)

In 1976, NOAA, a division of the United States Department of Commerce, took delivery of two new P-3s. On the Lockheed assembly line, these airframes were outwardly built as stock Orions but that is where the similarity ends. Designated WP-3Ds, the aircraft feature a beefed-up cabin floor designed to hold a variety of on-board instrumentation. The result is a highly advanced research aircraft. Currently based at McDill Air Force Base in Florida, the aircraft also fly in cooperation with other research organizations, both domestic and foreign. Whether tracking global weather patterns, arctic ice formations or penetrating a hurricane, the WP-3Ds are not scheduled for replacement in the near future.

Operated by Nordair on behalf of the Canadian Department of Environment, 188C CF-NAY (msn 1113) flew ice reconnaissance missions.
(Gary Vincent; Harry Sievers Collection)

C-GNDZ (msn 1111), with updated colors following a merger with Canadian Pacific, but still wearing Nordair titles.
(Pierre Langlois; Harry Sievers Collection)

Registered HX-CFE and later HX-HEB with the Bank of Mexico, msn 1056 migrated to Transafrik in December 1987. (Keith Armes)

Owned by FM Productions, Inc., 188C N42FM (msn 1077) supported a tour by the group Santana. (Harry Sievers Collection)

N6118A (msn 1072), owned by McCulloch International, was used for a Rolling Stones tour. (Gianfranco Beting)

N5017K (msn 1031) painted up for an Alice Cooper tour. (Airliners Collection)

Originally part of the defunct Capital Airlines order and bought by PSA, 188C N595KR (msn 1130) was leased by King Resources in the late 1960s. (Terry Waddington Collection)

Among the few Electras fitted with a corporate interior, msn 1112 is seen at Burbank in 1980. This aircraft was leased to Cathedral of Tomorrow and apparently operated on behalf of Christian ministers including Rex Humbard (see page 118).
(Jukka Kauppinen; Jon Proctor Collection)

Aerobureau's plans for Electra flying with N667F (msn 1131) never came to fruition. (Bob Shane)

Although not a hull loss, Reeve Aleutian's N1968R (msn 2007) was heavily damaged on June 8, 1983, when it lost the Number Four propeller and reduction gearbox en route from Cold Bay, Alaska, to Seattle. As the prop departed the aircraft, it ripped a large hole in the fuselage bottom, jamming some control cables and completely severing others. Captain James Gibson and his crew brought the crippled plane back to a safe landing at Anchorage despite limited control authority, a damaged brake system and the inability to change throttle settings. (Tom Verges, Sr.)

In addition to the accidents described in Chapter Three, the following is a review of subsequent hull losses. Photo inset accident dates have been added for reference.

June 12, 1961; KLM Flight 823
(msn 2019 – PH-LLM)

The KLM flight crashed while on a night visual approach to Cairo International Airport, Egypt, killing 20 of the 36 people on board. The weather consisted of a 2,500-foot broken ceiling with six miles of visibility. The captain was blamed for "inattention to his instruments during the landing approach," which was conducted at an abnormally high rate of descent.

September 17, 1961; Northwest Flight 711
(msn 1142 – N137US)

On climbout from Chicago-O'Hare, Northwest Flight 711 began a right turn that continued to increase until, at 90 degrees of bank, the aircraft descended and crashed. There were no survivors among the 37 passengers and crew. The loss of control was caused by an improperly installed aileron boost assembly. Garbled radio transmissions appear to indicate that the crew attempted to disconnect the aileron boost system and manually roll the aircraft upright. Although not proven, it is believed that there was no control response to the crew's action.

August 6, 1962; American Flight 414
(msn 1019 – N6102A)

The American Airlines Electra skidded off the right side of the runway at McGee-Tyson Airport, Knoxville, Tennessee, following an approach in thunderstorms and heavy rain. It then impacted on a newly constructed taxiway, tearing off the right main landing gear and halting after separation of the

right wing. Of the 72 people on board there was only one minor injury. The cause of the accident was found to be improper cross-wind landing technique resulting in loss of control.

March 27, 1965; Tasman Empire Airways, Ltd.
(msn 2011 – ZK-TEC)

TEAL crew members were operating this Electra on a training hop when it crashed while landing at Whenuapai Airport, New Zealand, after failing to arrest the sink rate following a steep approach. The aircraft departed the end of the runway and burned but there were no fatalities.

April 22, 1966; American Flyers Flight 280D
(msn 1136 – N183H)

This non-scheduled passenger flight, flown on contract for the Military Airlift Command, encountered poor weather on arrival at AFA's Ardmore, Oklahoma base. After missing one approach, the crew was attempting a visual, circling maneuver when the Electra struck a hill, killing 83 of the 98 aboard. Although it could not be verified, there was speculation that the captain, AFA founder Reed Pigman, may have suffered a heart attack.

April 22, 1966

AFA's N183H (msn 1136) at New York-JFK, three years prior to its demise. (Harry Sievers)

December 24, 1971

OB-R-941 (msn 1086), the second LANSA Electra hull loss. (Harry Sievers Collection)

February 16, 1967; Garuda Flight 708
(msn 2021 – PK-GLB)

Marginal weather greeted the Garuda Indonesia Airlines flight on its arrival at Manado, Indonesia. The crew flew a very erratic approach that almost resulted in the aircraft stalling. Instead, a hard landing followed, collapsing the undercarriage and setting the airliner aflame. There were 22 passenger fatalities and 70 survivors.

May 3, 1968; Braniff Flight 352
(msn 1099 – N9707C)

With 85 passengers and crew, Flight 352 departed from Houston on a late-afternoon service bound for Dallas. En route, the flight encountered an area of severe thunderstorms and was allowed by Air Traffic Control (ATC) to deviate and descend. The crew finally asked for and was permitted to execute a 180-degree turn.

It appears that the pilots lost control of the Electra and in an attempt to recover from an unusual attitude, overstressed the aircraft to the point of destruction. There were no survivors. A marketing program in effect offered Braniff passengers rebates for late arrivals, and some went so far as to speculate that the crew was trying to "beat the clock."

February 5, 1970; VARIG
(msn 1049 – PP-VJP)

This arriving flight landed short of the runway at Porto Alegre, Brazil, and collapsed the right main landing gear. There were no fatalities, but the aircraft was written off.

August 9, 1970; LANSA
(msn 1106 – OB-R-939)

After experiencing a Number Three engine failure on takeoff at Cuzco, Peru, the Electra began a steep left turn at low altitude and crashed during the bank. There was but one survivor among the 100 passengers and crew.

August 24, 1970;
Logair Flight 9524
(msn 2012 – N855U)

Universal Airlines was operating its Electra freighter on behalf of Logair when it crashed on takeoff, just after gear retraction, sliding 2,600 feet down the runway at Hill Air Force Base, Ogden, Utah. Crew members stated that even with two pilots on the controls and full nose-up trim, they were unable to stop the descent. Improperly set flaps or a control rigging problem was speculated. There were no fatalities.

December 24, 1971;
LANSA Flight 508
(msn 1086 – OB-R-941)

Only 40 minutes after departure from Lima, Peru, the flight encountered a severe storm and was believed struck by lightning, setting the aircraft on fire; it crashed into the jungle near Puerto Inca. Although the cause was not determined, it seems the Electra experienced a structural failure after the crew initiated extreme maneuvers as a result of an in-flight upset. All but one person of the 92 aboard died.

Amazingly, the sole survivor was a 17-year old girl who built a makeshift raft and navigated down a river to the nearest habitation during a 10-day ordeal. She survived on a Christmas cake brought on the flight as a gift for her father.

January 9, 1972; Air Manila International
(msn 1021 – PI-C1060)

During a crew training flight, the aircraft ran off the end of the runway at Pasay City, Philippines, and was destroyed. There were no casualties.

March 19, 1972; Universal Airlines
(msn 2001 – N851U)

Descending for landing at Hill AFB, Utah, the Electra freighter experienced a low-oil warning on the Number Two propeller. The crew responded by shutting down the associated engine, but the propeller would not feather. On landing it separated from the aircraft and fragments punctured a fuel tank. The ensuing fire destroyed the aircraft; no fatalities.

August 27, 1973; Aerocondor Colombia
(msn 1115 – HK-777)

After takeoff from Bogota, Colombia, the Electra crashed into a hill, killing all 42 crew and passengers.

October 30, 1974; Pan Arctic Oil Co.
(msn 1141 – CF-PAB)

The non-scheduled passenger flight crashed into the ice and water two miles short of the runway near Rae Point, in Canada. All but two aboard were killed.

November 5, 1974; Reeve Aleutian Airways
(msn 1118 – N7140C)

The 188PF was destroyed in a hangar fire at Reeve's Anchorage, Alaska, headquarters.

March 19, 1972

N851U (msn 2001), destroyed by fire after a prop separation on landing. (Harry Sievers Collection)

December 11, 1974; Fairbanks Air Service
(msn 1064 – N400FA)

Upon landing at Deadhorse, Alaska, with a full cargo load of diesel fuel, the Fairbanks Air 188AF veered off the left edge of the runway. The Number Two engine broke loose and the aircraft caught fire. The crew escaped uninjured.

April 30, 1975

N283F (msn 1089) served with ONA prior to Zantop. (Harry Sievers)

April 30, 1975; Zantop International
(msn 1089 – N283F)

In another Deadhorse, Alaska, accident, the Electra freighter's left wing separated from the airframe following a hard landing. There were no fatalities as the aircraft came to a stop inverted and beyond the left side of the runway.

July 10, 1975; Aerocondor Colombia
(msn 1087 – HK-1976)

Shortly after liftoff from Bogota, Colombia, the Electra freighter settled back to the ground and struck a parked aircraft. Both burned but there were no deaths.

March 12, 1976; Great Northern Airlines
(msn 1059 – N401FA)

Landing at Udrivik Lake, Alaska, the crew found the braking action was insufficient to stop and put their aircraft into a ground loop. The right main landing gear buckled and a fire ensued. No one was seriously injured.

June 4, 1976; Air Manila International Flight 702
(msn 1007 – RP-C1061)

There were no survivors of this flight that crashed shortly after liftoff at Agana, Guam. The Number Three engine had failed on the takeoff roll. Choosing to continue, the crew apparently raised the flaps too soon. The Electra struck a hill at an altitude of 100 feet.

July 2, 1976; Eastern Air Lines
(msn 1055 – N5531)

The Electra, assigned to the Air-Shuttle, was destroyed by a bomb while parked overnight at Logan International Airport, Boston, Massachusetts.

March 31, 1977; Nordair·
(msn 1132 – CF-NAZ)

Parked at the Canadian Forces Base at Summerside, Canada, the Nordair 188C was badly damaged when an errant Royal Canadian Air Force CL-28 military aircraft crashed in to it while landing. (Note: portions of this airframe was used in part to rebuild msn 1111.)

June 30, 1977; Cooperativa de Montecillos
(msn 1105 – N126US)

The 188CF freighter crashed about 65 miles offshore from Panama. There were no survivors among the four occupants.

July 6, 1977; Fleming International
(msn 1076 – N280F)

Following an aborted takeoff due to the Number Two engine auto-feathering, the crew again tried to depart Lambert International Airport, St. Louis, Missouri. On the second try, Number Two was reduced to idle power. After liftoff, the aircraft veered to the left and crashed. All three crew members were killed.

January 5, 1979; Great Northern Airlines
(msn 1127 – N403GN)

Landing on the North Slope of Alaska, the 188PF touched down short of the runway, causing the left main landing gear and wing to separate from the aircraft. There were no casualties.

June 4, 1976

Originally N5502 with Eastern, AMI flew msn 1007 for nearly three years before its loss with all aboard. (Harry Sievers Collection)

July 2, 1976

Destroyed by a bomb in 1976, Eastern's N5531 (msn 1055) was subsequently scrapped at Logan International Airport, Boston. (Fred Krueger; Jon Proctor Collection)

March 31, 1977

Seen at Montreal in May 1976, highly modified msn 1132 was struck a year later while parked. (Steve Bailey; Harry Sievers Collection)

July 6, 1977

Despite persistent problems with the Number Two engine, the crew of Electra freighter N280F (msn 1076) persisted, with tragic results. (Eddy Gual)

November 18, 1979; Transamerica Flight 3N18
(msn 2016 – N859U)

The all-cargo Electra departed Hill AFB, Utah, on a freight run to Nellis AFB in Nevada. Flying under instrument flight conditions, the crew notified ATC of an electrical problem and requested to return to Hill and execute a "no-gyro" instrument approach. While changing vectors, the crew evidently lost control of the aircraft which entered a steep descent with a marked increase in airspeed. During the recovery attempt, the stress limits of the 188CF were exceeded and it broke up in flight over Granger, Utah, killing the three crew members.

February 2, 1980; TACA
(msn 1069 – YS-07C)

This 188AF burned on the ground after a wing caught fire at San Salvador, El Salvador. There were no injuries.

January 8, 1981; SAHSA
(msn 1018 – HR-SAW)

The Electra landed at La Aurora Airport, Guatemala City, with one engine shut down. After deplaning the passengers, it departed on a three-engine ferry flight to Honduras for repairs. Shortly after takeoff, the crew reported hydraulic system malfunctions and difficulty in controlling the airliner, which crashed during an attempted return to the airport. The cause was determined to be an electrical failure causing a drop in hydraulic pressure and resultant loss of control. Six crew members died in the crash.

March, 21 1982; Zantop
(msns 1009 & 1022 –
N5504 & N5516)

The two 188AF Electra Freighters were damaged beyond repair at Macon, Georgia, when the maintenance hangar in which they were housed collapsed in severe weather.

May 30, 1984; Zantop
(msn 1034 – N5523)

En route from Baltimore to its Detroit-Willow Run Airport base at night, the Electra freighter crew reported a failure of the attitude indicating system. Although at least one indicator may have been presenting correct information, control was lost and the aircraft broke up in flight over at Chalkhill, Pennsylvania, when the crew members did not detect the onset of a dive from altitude. There was no standby attitude indicator installed. All four crew members died.

January 9, 1985; TPI International
(msn 1044 – N357Q)

Arriving in the early morning at Kansas City Municipal Airport, Missouri, the crew shot an approach in poor weather conditions. Upon breaking out they found themselves too high and were given clearance to circle the field. ATC then informed the crew that they appeared to be lining up for the wrong airport. During the climbout the aircraft stalled and spiraled to the ground. There was no evidence of mechanical abnormalities or cargo shifting. Three fatal injuries resulted.

January 5, 1979

N403GN (msn 1127) is seen nearly six years prior to its demise. N74191, shown being prepared for Pacific Western, became CF-PAK. (Harry Sievers Collection)

February 2, 1980

YS-07C (msn 1069) of TACA succumbed to a ground fire with no human casualties.
(Harry Sievers Collection)

March 21, 1982

A collapsed hangar claimed Zantop Electra freighters N5504 and
N5516. (both Harry Sievers Collection)

May 30, 1984

N5523 (msn 1034) broke up in flight. (Jon Proctor Collection)

January 21, 1985;
Galaxy Airlines Flight 203
(msn 1121 – N5532)

The Electra was behind schedule when it departed from Reno, Nevada, with 71 passengers and crew. Shortly after liftoff the captain requested an immediate return to the airport, reporting heavy vibrations and the need to get the aircraft back on the ground. During the turn, the pilot reduced power on all four engines, apparently in response to the vibration. Flight 203 then descended and crashed, resulting in fatal injuries to all but one on board. The vibration was attributed to an improperly secured access door.

January 29, 1985; Galaxy Airlines
(msn 2009 – N854U)

After departing from Marietta, Georgia, the 188CF's partially retracted right main landing gear became jammed. The flight was diverted to Dobbins AFB and landed with only the nose and left main gear fully extended. On touchdown, the Electra veered off the runway, where a small fire near the right wheel well was quickly extinguished and the crew exited without injury. The airframe was damaged beyond economical repair.

November 30, 1985;
Mandala Airlines
(msn 2008 – PK-RLG)

On approach to Panang, Malaysia, the right main landing gear apparently separated from the 188C. The crew diverted to Medan, Indonesia, and successfully completed a gear-up landing. There were no fatalities; however, the airframe was scrapped.

February 5, 1986; TRAMACO
(msn 1045 – 9Q-CWT)

This 188AF was damaged beyond repair in an off-airport forced landing at Kasongo-Lunda, Zaire, about 120 miles from Kinshasa. Two passengers were killed.

September 12, 1988; TAME
(msn 1052 – HC-AZY)

While departing from Lago Agrio, Ecuador, on a three-engine ferry flight, the Electra experienced an additional power plant failure. With two engines out on one side and control lost, the aircraft veered left and crashed. There were no survivors.

January 21, 1985

There was only one survivor of the Galaxy accident in January 1985. (Bruce Drum)

January 29, 1985

N854U (msn 2009) was still wearing this basic livery when it crash-landed in Georgia. (Harry Sievers Collection)

November 30, 1985

PK-RLG was applied to msn 2008 just before its transfer from Nomads to Mandala, in late 1981. It was scrapped four years later, following a gear-up landing. (Harry Sievers Collection)

September 12, 1988

During a three-engine takeoff, HC-AZY (msn 1052) experienced yet another engine failure. The aircraft left the runway and burned. (Peter Legate)

September 4, 1989; TAME
(msn 2004 – HC-AZJ)

After takeoff from Quito, Ecuador, the Electra's left main landing gear failed to retract. The crew elected to execute a belly landing at Taura AFB. The landing was successful with no major injuries. Investigation revealed that a failed landing gear door support rod jammed the doors and landing gear strut. The airframe was damaged beyond economical repair.

March 21, 1990; TAN Honduras
(msn 1134 – HR-TNL)

Approaching Tegucigalpa Airport, Honduras, in poor weather, the 188CF impacted the side of a hill, well below the recommended safe altitude. All on board were killed.

TAN's Electra freighter HR-TNL (msn 1134), crashed on approach for landing. (Avimage)

N5517 (msn 1023) suffered a cockpit fire while parked. Considered beyond economical repair, it was scrapped. (Harry Sievers Collection)

Photographed in 1990 while with LAP, msn 1080 crashed at Jamba, Angola. (Bill Hough)

July, 14, 1990; TPI International
(msn 1096 – N4464F)

On a flight from Aruba to Panama, the Number Three reduction gearbox failed on the 188CF. The propeller subsequently separated and struck the Number Four propeller. Fragments cut through the fuselage and damaged the Number Two engine, which was secured. With only the Number One power plant on line, no brakes, limited hydraulics and stiff flight controls, the crew made a successful landing at Aruba's Reina Beatrix Airport. There were no injuries but the aircraft was damaged beyond economical repair.

August 1992;
New Air Charter Service
(msn 1111 – 9Q-CRY)

The aircraft was reportedly damaged beyond economical repair; no further details available.

April 14, 1993; Zantop International
(msn 1023 – N5517)

While sitting quietly on the ramp at Willow Run Airport, Detroit, Michigan, the air conditioning duct overheated, setting the cockpit aflame. Considered beyond economical repair, the airframe was sold for scrap except for the engines and props which Zantop retained as spares.

January 21, 1994; Trans Service Airlift
(msn 1126 – 9Q-CCV)

The Electra was damaged beyond repair when the nose gear collapsed on landing at Kinshasa, Zaire. The occupants were uninjured.

July 1994; Filair
(msn 1139 – 9Q-CGD)

This aircraft, it is reported, crashed in Angola; no other details have been obtained.

March 13, 1995; Blue Airlines
(msn 1119 – 9Q-CDG)

The 188A was damaged beyond repair when it crashed on landing at N'Djili Airport, Kinshasa, Zaire. There were no fatalities.

December 18, 1995; Trans Service Airlift
(msn 1080 – 9Q-CRR)

Mystery still surrounds this takeoff accident of this 188C at Jamba, Angola, which killed 141 of the 144 people on board. Despite being obviously overloaded, the flight, which may have been chartered by a rebel movement, could have been shot down. There is also speculation that the aircraft was being used to smuggle diamonds out of Angola via Zaire.

Hull Losses

(Listed By Manufacturer's Serial Number)

msn	Original Registration	Last Registration	Operator	Date	Location	Comments
1007	N5502	RP-C1061	Air Manila International	06/04/76	Agana, Guam	takeoff
1009	N5504		Zantop	03/21/82	Macon, GA	hangar collapse
1015	N6101A		American	02/03/59	New York, NY	landing
1018	N5513	HR-SAW	SAHSA	01/08/81	Guatemala City, Guatemala	takeoff
1019	N6102A		American	08/06/62	Knoxville, TN	landing
1021	N5515	PI-C1060	Air Manila International	01/09/72	Pasay City, Philippines	crew training
1022	N5516		Zantop	03/21/82	Macon, GA	hangar collapse
1023	N5517		Zantop	04/14/93	Detroit, MI	ground fire
1034	N5523		Zantop	05/30/84	Chalkhill, PA	en route
1044	VH-RMC	N357Q	TPI International	01/09/85	Kansas City, MO	approach
1045	N5528	9Q-CWT	TRAMACO	02/05/86	near Kinshasa, Zaire	forced landing
1049	N6110A	PP-VJP	VARIG	02/05/70	Porto Alegre, Brazil	landing
1052	N9702C	HC-AZY	TAME	09/12/88	Lago Agrio, Ecuador	takeoff
1055	N5531		Eastern	07/02/76	Boston, MA	sabotage
1057	N121US		Northwest	03/17/60	Tell City, IN	en route
1059	N5002K	N401FA	Great Northern	03/12/76	Lake Udrivik, AK	landing
1062	N5533		Eastern	10/04/60	Boston-Logan	takeoff
1064	N5003K	N400FA	Fairbanks Air Service	12/11/74	Deadhorse, AK	landing
1069	VH-TLB	YS-07C	TACA	02/02/80	San Salvador, El Salvador	ground fire
1076	N5004K	N280F	Fleming International	07/06/77	St. Louis, MO	takeoff
1080	N5539	9Q-CRR	Trans Service Airlift	12/18/95	northern Angola	unknown
1086	N9704C	OB-R-941	LANSA	12/24/71	Puerto Inca, Peru	en route
1087	N7138C	HK-1976	Aerocondor	07/10/75	Bogota, Colombia	takeoff
1089	N5007K	N283F	Zantop	04/30/75	Deadhorse, AK	landing
1090	N9705C		Braniff	09/29/59	Buffalo, TX	en route
1096	N5009K	N4464F	TPI International	07/14/90	Aruba	en route
1099	N9707C		Braniff	05/03/68	Dawson, TX	en route
1105	N126US		Coop. de Montecillos	06/30/77	Offshore Panama	en route
1106	N9708C	OB-R-939	LANSA	08/09/70	Cuzco, Peru	takeoff
1111	N128US	9Q-CRY	New ACS	08/—/92	unknown	unknown
1115	N6125A	HK-777	Aerocondor	08/27/73	Bogota, Colombia	takeoff
1117	N6127A		American	09/14/60	New York, NY	landing
1118	N7140C		Reeve Aleutian	11/05/74	Anchorage, AK	hangar fire
1119	N6128A	9Q-CDG	Blue Airlines	03/13/95	Kinshasa, Zaire	landing
1121	N6130A	N5532	Galaxy	01/21/85	Reno, NV	approach
1126	N6135A	9Q-CCV	Trans Service Airlift	01/21/94	Kinshasa, Zaire	landing
1127	N7141C	N403GN	Great Northern	01/05/79	Alaska North Slope	landing
1132	N132US	CF-NAZ	Nordair	03/31/77	Summerside, PEI, Canada	ground collision
1134	N9710C	HR-TNL	TAN	03/21/90	Tegucigalpa, Honduras	en route
1136	N183H		American Flyers	04/22/66	Ardmore, OK	approach
1139	N135US	9Q-CGD`	Filair	07/—/94	Angola	unknown
1141	N136US	CF-PAB	Pan Arctic Oil	10/30/74	Rae Point, NWT, Canada	landing
1142	N137US		Northwest	09/17/61	Chicago, IL	takeoff
2001	PH-LLA	N851U	Universal	03/19/72	Hill AFB, UT	landing
2004	VH-ECB	HC-AZJ	TAME	09/04/89	Taura AFB, Ecuador	landing
2008	VH-ECD	PK-RLG	Mandala	11/30/85	Medan, Indonesia	landing
2009	PH-LLD	N854U	Galaxy	01/29/85	Dobbins AFB, GA	landing
2011	ZK-TEC		TEAL	03/27/65	Whenuapai, New Zealand	landing
2012	PH-LLE	N855U	Universal	08/24/70	Hill AFB, UT	takeoff
2016	PH-LLI	N859U	Transamerica	11/18/79	near Granger, UT	en route
2019	PH-LLM		KLM	06/12/61	Cairo, Egypt	landing
2021	PK-GLB		Garuda	02/16/67	Menado, Indonesia	landing

PP-VJM (msn 1025) was donated by VARIG to the Campos Dos Afonsos Airspace Museum in Brazil. (Gianfranco Beting)

Inevitably, the number of Electras in service is slowly dwindling. In light of this fact, it may be comforting to know that at least three examples are preserved in museums. Although in the greatly altered form as the prototype P-3 Orion, msn 1003 is extant in the Naval Aviation Museum at Pensacola, Florida.

Two 188s are on display in South America. One, an ex-VARIG airliner in Brazil, was donated by that airline. Likewise, the Argentine Navy has seen fit to contribute one of its hard-working Electras to a museum. Is it possible that some enthusiast group may keep an Electra active for the airshow circuit? Infinitely more costly to maintain and fly than a DC-3 or even a DC-4, this proposition is doubtful. Like many expensive machines, the Electra must be turning a profit to operate.

What does the future hold? Unfortunately, there are trends that indicate the old bird is getting more and more difficult to maintain and keep airworthy. One problem is the propeller, which can be overhauled just so many times before it must be declared non-repairable. Those companies flying the 188 today know where the remaining, serviceable props are located. An obvious question is whether or not a P-3 propeller can be retrofitted to its civilian counterpart. The answer is yes, but this transition requires substantial modification, and many feel it is not worth the money.

Another area of concern is the wing planks. Recently a North American operator found out the hard way that these components are starting to show signs of wear. This firm purchased an Electra from a South American firm and ferried the airplane to its home base, where closer inspection revealed cracked planks. Fortunately, replacement parts were located. However, as with propellers, there are only so many wing planks left; to fabricate new ones would be cost prohibitive.

Finally, the demise of almost any older aircraft often comes in the form of corrosion. One company recently turned a 188 over to a repair station for scheduled heavy maintenance, only to find that corrosion had so inundated the airframe that it was beyond economical repair.

For the immediate future, the Electra's role seems secure. Most of the companies operating the type find them to be viable when properly maintained. During the turboprop's 40-year history, few have remained idle for a long period of time. Despite parts shortages, the Lockheed Electra continues to earn its keep and will, it is hoped, gracefully fly well into the next century.

Henry Tenby

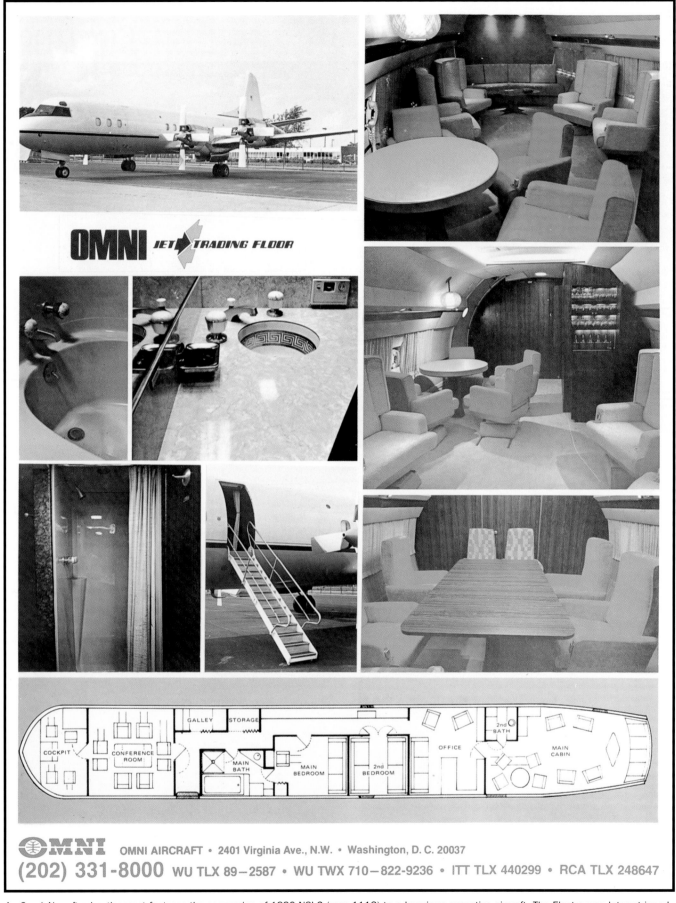

An Omni Aircraft advertisement features the conversion of 188C N8LG (msn 1112) to a luxurious executive aircraft. The Electra was later stripped of its amenities and relegated to cargo flying. (Todd Duhnke Collection)

Appendix I • Turboprop Lineup

Manufacturer	Lockheed (USA)	Lockheed (USA) Armstrong (UK)	Vickers-Armstrong (UK)	Vickers-Armstrong (UK)	Vickers	Douglas (USA)	Bristol (UK)	Ilyushin (USSR)
Model	188A Electra	188C Electra	Viscount 700	Viscount 802	Vanguard 953	DC-7D	Britannia 300	IL-18D
First Flight	Dec. 6, 1957	July 1, 1959	Aug. 28, 1950	July 27, 1956	Jan. 20, 1959	(not built)	Aug. 16, 1952	July 1957
Accommodations	66–98	66–98	40–59	44–70	97–139	cargo only	133	122
Power Plants	4 x General Motors Allison 501D-13 (or D-13A, or D-15)	4 x General Motors Allison 501D-13 (or D-13A, or D-15)	4 x Rolls-Royce Dart 504	4 x Rolls-Royce Dart 510	4 x Rolls-Royce Tyne Mk 512	4 x Rolls-Royce Tyne	4 x Bristol Prodeus Type 755	4 x Ivchenko AI-20M
Horsepower	501D-13/3,750 eshp 501D-15/4,050 eshp	501D-13/3,750 eshp 501D-15/4,050 eshp	1,400 shp	1,600 shp	5,050 shp	unknown	4,120 eshp	4,250 shp
Fuel Capacity	5,360 U.S. gallons	6,520 U.S. gallons	1,720 Imp. gallons	1,720 Imp. gallons	5,130 Imp. gallons	unknown	6,670 Imp. gallons	6,599 Imp. gal
Dimensions								
Wingspan	99 feet	99 feet	94 feet	94 feet	118 feet	127ft, 6in	142ft, 3.5in	122ft, 8.5in
Length	104ft, 6in	104ft, 6in	81ft, 2in	85 feet	118 feet	112ft, 3in	124ft, 3in	117ft, 9in
Height	32ft, 10in	32ft, 10in	26ft, 9in	26ft, 9in	34ft, 11in	31ft, 8in	37ft, 6in	33ft, 4in
Weights								
Max takeoff	113,000 lbs	116,000 lbs	52,500 lbs	63,000 lbs	146,500 lbs	170,000 lbs	160,000 lbs	141,000 lbs
Max landing	95,650 lbs	95,650 lbs	50,000 lbs	58,500 lbs	130,500 lbs	unknown	130,000 lbs	unknown
Empty (domestic)	56,000 lbs	56,000 lbs	32,330 lbs	40,776 lbs	82,500 lbs	unknown	86,900 lbs	77,160 lbs
Empty (overseas)	57,000 lbs	57,000 lbs	N/A	N/A	N/A	N/A	N/A	N/A
Payload	21,638 lbs	21,638 lbs	12,500 lbs	13,224 lbs	37,000 lbs	70,000 lbs	30,000 lbs	29,750 lbs
Performance								
Max Airspeed	448 mph	448 mph (at 12,000ft)	331 mph (at 12,000ft)	325 mph (at 25,000ft)	425 mph (at 20,000ft)	unknown (at 20,000ft)	390 mph	419 mph
Cruise Airspeed	405 mph	405 mph (at 22,000ft)	311 mph (at 22,000ft)	314 mph (at 25,000ft)	402 mph (at 20,000ft)	428 mph (at 25,000ft)	346 mph	388 mph
Maximum range	2,770 miles	3,460 miles	variable depending on configuration	1,035 miles	2,570 miles	2,086 miles	3,860 miles	3,508 miles

Appendix II
ELECTRA OPERATORS

Note: The following list contains companies that actually flew the Lockheed Electra. It does not denote whether or not the operator actually owned or leased the aircraft. Also, not included are leasing firms that never flew but simply traded in airliners.

Adventurers Travel Club - U.S.
Aero Union - U.S. (P-3 tankers)
Aerocarga - Mexico
Aeroclub International - U.S.
Aerocondor – Aerovias Condor de Colombia
   - Colombia
Aerocosta - Colombia
Aeronauts International - U.S.
Aeroservices de California - Mexico
Aerovias - Guatemala
Air Andes International - Ecuador
Air Atlantique - U.K.
Air Bridge Carriers - U.K.
Air California - U.S.
Air Ceylon - Ceylon (Sri Lanka)
Air Florida - U.S.
Air Holiday - U.S.
Air Manila International - Philippines
Air New Zealand Ltd. (formerly TEAL
   - Tasman Empire Airways) - New Zealand
Air Spray Ltd. - Canada
Airtrust Singapore - Singapore
ALM Antillian Airlines - Dutch Antilles
Alice Cooper - U.S.
Allison Division of General Motors - U.S.
Amerer Air - Austria
American Airlines - U.S.
American Flyers Airline - U.S.
American Jet Industries - U.S.
Ansett–ANA - Australia
ANSHA – Aerovias Nacionales de Honduras, S.A.
   - Honduras
APEL – Aerolineas Petroleras del Llano S.A.
   - Colombia
APSA – Aero Servicios Puntarenas S.A. - Costa Rica
Argentine Navy - Argentina
Atlantic Airlines - U.K.
Atlantic Cargo - U.K.
Blue Airlines - Zaire
Braniff Airways (Braniff International) - U.S.
California Republican Party - U.S.
CAM Air International - U.S.
Canadien Airlines - Canada
Carib West Airways - Barbados
Cathay Pacific Airways Ltd. - Hong Kong
Cathedral of Tomorrow - U.S.
Century 2000 - U.S.
Channel Express Air Services - U.K.
Charrak Air - Australia
Conair - Canada
COPA – Compania Panamena de Aviacion - Panama

Cooperitiva de Montecillos - Panama
Cruzeiro – Servicios Aereos Cruzeiro do Sul, Ltda.
   - Brazil
Dave Clark Five - U.S.
Dominicana – Compania de Aviacion
   - Dominican Republic
Eagle Air - Iceland
Eastern Air Lines - U.S.
Ecuatoriana – Compania Ecuatoriana de Aviacion
   - Ecuador
Evergreen International Airlines - U.S.
FAA – Federal Aviation Administration - U.S.
Fairbanks Air Service - U.S.
Falconair Charter AB - Sweden
Falcon Aviation - Sweden
Fiesta Air - U.S.
Filair - Zaire
Flamingo Airlines - Bahamas
Fleming International - U.S.
FM Productions - U.S.
FPE Travel Club - U.S.
Fred Olsen Airtransport Ltd. – Fred Olsens Flyselskap
A/S - Norway
Galaxy Airlines - U.S.
Garuda Indonesian Airways - Indonesia
General American Development Corporation - U.S.
Great Northern Airlines - U.S.
Groupe Litho Mobiti Aviation - Zaire
Gulf Air Transport - U.S.
Guyana Airways - Guyana
Hawaiian Airlines - U.S.
Holiday Airlines - U.S.
Holiday Wings - U.S.
Honduran Government - Honduras
Hunting Cargo Airlines Ltd. - Ireland
Hunting Cargo Airlines Ltd. - U.K.
IBERIA – Lineas Aereas de Espana - Spain
Imperial Oil Ltd. - Canada
Indian Ocean Airlines - Australia
Interlink of Congo
Intermountain Aviation - U.S.
INAIR – Internacional de Aviacion - Panama
International Jetair Ltd. - Canada
Interstate Airlines - U.S.
Iona National Airways Ltd. - Ireland
Iscargo - Iceland
Jet Set Travel Club - U.S.
Johnson Flying Service - U.S.
Jupiter Airways - U.S.
King Resources - U.S.
KLM Royal Dutch Airlines - Netherlands
LAB – Lloyd Aereo Boliviano S.A. - Bolivia
LACSA – Lineas Aereas Costaricenses S.A.
   - Costa Rica
Lakewood Properties - U.S.
LANSA – Lineas Aereas Nacionales S.A. - Peru
LAP – Lineas Aereas Paraguayas - Paraguay

Legion Express - U.S.
Lockheed Aircraft Corporation - U.S.
Logair - U.S.
Los Angeles Dodgers - U.S.
Lynden Air Cargo - U.S.
Mandala Airlines - Indonesia
Martinair Holland - Netherlands
McCarthy Presidential Committee - U.S.
McCulloch International Airlines - U.S.
Mexican Air Force - Mexico
Mexican Government (Banco de Mexico) - Mexico
Muskie Travel Committee - U.S.
National Airlines - U.S.
NASA – National Aeronautics & Space Administration
    - U.S.
NCAR – National Center for Atmospheric Research
    - U.S.
New Air Charter Service - Zaire
Nomads - U.S.
Nordair Ltd. - Canada
Nordic-Air Services - Norway
Northwest Airlines - U.S.
Norwegian Military - Norway
NWT Air – Northwest Territorial Airways Ltd. - Canada
ONA – Overseas National Airways - U.S.
Pacific American Airlines - U.S.
Pacific Southwest Airlines - U.S.
Pacific Western Airlines - Canada
Panama Air Force – Fuerza Aerea Panamena - Panama
Pan Arctic Oil Company Ltd. - Canada
Pelican Express - U.S.
Persian Air Service - Iran
Pigatari S.A. - Brazil
Ports-of-Call Travel Club - U.S.
QANTAS Empire Airways - Australia
Renown Aviation - U.S.
Reeve Aleutian Airways - U.S.
Royal Air Lao - Laos
RPS Investments - U.S.
SAHSA – Servicio Aereo de Honduras, S.A.
    - Honduras
SAM Colombia – Sociedad Aeronautica
    de Medellin Consolidada - Colombia
San Diego Padres - U.S.

Saturn Airways - U.S.
Shillelaghs of Washington - U.S.
Spirit of America Airlines - U.S.
Sports Aloft - U.S.
Southeast Airlines - U.S.
STAF – Servicios de Transportes Aereos Fueguinos
    - Argentina
Sterling Airways Sweden AB - Denmark
Summit Airlines - U.S.
TACA International Airlines S.A. - El Salvador
TAM-Bolivia – Transportes Aereos Militares - Bolivia
TAME-Ecuador – Transportes Aereos Militares
Ecuatorianos - Ecuador
TAN - Honduras
    – Transportes Aereas Nacionales S.A. - Honduras
TPI International Airways - U.S.
TRAMCO – Transports & Manutentions Commerciaux
    - Zaire
Transafrik - Sao Tome & Principe
Trans Air Cargo - U.S.
Transamerica Airlines - U.S.
Transapel Express (Transapel S.A.) - Colombia
Trans Arctic Airlines - U.S.
Trans-Australia Airlines – TAA - Australia
Transbrasil Linhas Aereas S.A. - Brazil
Transcarga, S.A. - Costa Rica
Trans Continental Air Transport - U.S.
Trans International Airlines– TIA - U.S.
Trans Service Airlift - Zaire
U.S. Department of the Interior
U.S. Navy
Universal Airlines - U.S.
Utah Symphony Orchestra - U.S.
Vagabond Air Travel Club - U.S.
Valley Trading Company - U.S.
VARIG – Viacao Aerea Rio-Grandense S.A. - Brazil
Voyager 1000 Travel Club - U.S.
Western Airlines - U.S.
Winner Airways - U.S.
World Airline - Gambia
Zantop International Airlines - U.S.

Gianfranco Beting

LOCKHEED 188 PRODUCTION LIST

Determining the viability of the remaining Electra airframes is sometimes difficult. For the purposes of this chart, an airframe that is listed as **BU** has virtually no chance of ever flying again. An example is this is msn 1010 which, although a few parts still remain at Mojave, is basically scrap metal. On the other hand, msn 1082 is Still extant. Although it is currently being used for spares, there may be an outside chance it will fly once more. With regard to cargo conversions (**Cargo Conv**), some 188s were built

as A models and while undergoing modification were upgraded to C model status. These aircraft are listed here as CFs.

This chart is accurate as of October 1998. It should be noted that information on Electras in some parts of the world is sketchy at best. Any additions or corrections would be appreciated and should be addressed to the publisher.

Abbreviations:

msn	Manufacturer's Serial Number
BU	Broken up. Some components of these airframes may still exist.
WO	Written off, crashed or destroyed. See Chapters III & VI.

Cargo Conversions

AF	188A freighter
CF	188C freighter
PF	188A/C Combi psgr./freighter

Original Operators

AA	American Airlines
AN	Ansett–ANA
BN	Braniff International Airways
EA	Eastern Air Lines
FAA	Federal Aviation Administration
GA	Garuda Indonesian Airways
GM	Allison Division - General Motors
KL	KLM-Royal Dutch Airlines
LAC	Lockheed Aircraft Corporation
NA	National Airlines
NW	Northwest Airlines
PS	Pacific Southwest Airlines
QF	QANTAS
SA	Sports Aloft, Inc.
TE	Tasman Empire Airlines
TA	Trans-Australia Airlines
WA	Western Airlines

msn	model	First Flight	Del. Date	Original Operator	Registr	Cargo Conv.	Current Status	Current/Last Known Operator (Registration)	Notes
1001	A	12/06/57		LAC	N1881		BU		Oakland, CA; 1975. Prototype
1002	A	02/13/58		LAC	N1882		BU		Quito, Ecuador; 1981. Prototype
1003	A	08/19/58		LAC	N1883		Preserved		Naval Aviation Museum. Prototype
1004	A	04/10/58		LAC	N1884		BU		Quito, Ecuador; 1981. Prototype
1005	A	05/16/58	01/03/59	EA	N5501		BU		1977; for spares
1006	A	06/12/58	07/10/58	GM	N5501V			Air Spray (C-FVFH)	converted to tanker
1007	A	09/17/58	10/08/58	EA	N5502		WO		06/04/76; Agana, Guam
1008	A	10/02/58	10/20/58	EA	N5503		BU		1978; for spares
1009	A	10/11/58	11/02/58	EA	N5504	AF	WO		03/21/82; Macon, GA
1010	A	10/22/58	11/02/58	EA	N5505		BU		1982; Mojave, CA
1011	A	10/17/58	11/03/58	EA	N5506		BU		sections still at Mojave, CA
1012	A	10/26/58	11/14/58	EA	N5507	AF		Zantop (N5507)	stored; Detroit-Willow Run
1013	A	11/09/58	11/29/58	EA	N5509		BU		1980; for spares
1014	A	12/04/58	01/13/59	EA	N5510	AF		Zantop (N5510L)	stored; Detroit-Willow Run
1015	A	11/26/58	11/27/58	AA	N6101A		WO		02/03/59; New York, NY

msn	model	First Flight	Del. Date	Original Operator	Registr	Cargo Conv.	Current Status	Current/Last Known Operator (Registration)	Notes
1016	A	12/04/58	01/11/59	EA	N5511		BU		Tucson, AZ; 1980
1017	A	11/02/58	11/25/58	EA	N5512		AF	Zantop (N5512)	
1018	A	11/01/58	12/16/58	EA	N5513		WO		01/08/81; Guatemala City
1019	A	11/09/58	12/10/58	AA	N6102A		WO		08/06/62; Knoxville, TN
1020	A	01/26/59	02/13/59	EA	N5514		BU		1981; sections still at Mojave, CA
1021	A	01/06/59	02/02/59	EA	N5515		WO		01/09/72; Pasay City, Philippines
1022	A	01/01/59	01/19/59	EA	N5516	AF	WO		03/21/82; Macon, GA
1023	A	12/06/58	01/18/59	EA	N5517	AF	WO		04/14/93; Detroit-Willow Run
1024	A	12/28/58	01/04/59	AA	N6103A			Blue Airlines (9Q-CDK)	stored; Kinshasa, Zaire
1025	A	12/31/58	01/09/59	AA	N6104A		Preserved		Meseu Aerospacial, Brasil
1026	A	01/21/59	02/14/59	EA	N5518		BU		Jakarta, Indonesia
1027	A	12/13/58	01/23/59	AA	N6105A		BU		1974; for spares
1028	A	01/18/59	01/27/59	AA	N6106A			Honduran Govt. (HR-EMA)	
1029	A	02/12/59	02/26/59	EA	N5519		BU		1981; sections still at Mojave, CA
1030	A	02/19/59	02/28/59	EA	N5520		BU		
1031	A	01/31/59	02/05/59	AA	N6107A	AF	BU		1978; Miami, FL; for spares
1032	A	02/13/59	03/12/59	EA	N5521				stored; Asuncion, Paraguay
1033	A	01/22/59	02/03/59	EA	N5522	AF		Zantop (N5522)	stored; Detroit-Willow Run
1034	A	02/09/59	02/25/59	EA	N5523	AF	WO		05/30/84; Chalkhill, PA
1035	A	03/20/59	04/01/59	NA	N5001K	PF		Zantop (N341HA)	stored; Detroit-Willow Run
1036	A	02/09/59	02/26/59	EA	N5524			Renown Aviation (N351Q)	
1037	A	01/27/59	02/16/59	AA	N6108A		BU	Blue Airlines (9Q-CDI)	
1038	A	02/06/59	02/28/59	EA	N5525	AF		Zantop (N344HA)	
1039	A	02/13/59	02/27/59	AN	VH-RMA	AF		Amerer Air (N356Q)	
1040	A	04/08/59	04/29/59	BN	N9701C			Air Spray (C-GBKT)	converted to tanker
1041	A	02/01/59	02/27/59	AA	N6109A			Filair (9Q-CXU)	
1042	A	06/03/59	08/04/59	EA	N5526		BU		1975; Miami, FL
1043	A	03/10/59	04/16/59	EA	N5527	AF		Zantop (N346HA)	stored; Detroit-Willow Run
1044	A	11/01/59	02/05/60	AN	VH-RMC	AF	WO		01/09/85; Kansas City, MO
1045	A	03/20/59	04/27/59	EA	N5528	AF	WO		02/05/86; Kasongo-Luanda, Zaire
1046	A	04/30/59	05/20/59	WA	N7135C		BU		1986; Anchorage, AK
1047	A	02/28/59	04/01/59	AN	VH-RMB	AF	BU		11/96; Opa-locka, FL
1048	A	03/27/59	05/07/59	EA	N5529	AF		TRAMACO (9Q-CWR)	stored; Kinshasa, Zaire
1049	A	03/25/59	04/01/59	AA	N6110A		WO		02/05/70; Porto Alegre, Brazil
1050	A	04/08/59	04/16/59	AA	N6111A			Amerer Air (EL-WWS)	being broken up for parts
1051	A	04/15/59	04/22/59	AA	N6112A	PF		Mexican A.F. (XC-UTA)	stored; Seletar, Singapore
1052	A	03/16/59	05/06/59	BN	N9702C		WO		09/12/88; Lago Agrio, Ecuador
1053	A	04/23/59	05/20/59	EA	N5530	AF		Zantop (N343HA)	stored; Detroit-Willow Run
1054	A	04/22/59	04/30/59	AA	N6113A		BU		04/74; Miami, FL

msn	model	First Flight	Del. Date	Original Operator	Registr	Cargo Conv.	Current Status	Current/Last Known Operator (Registration)	Notes
1055	A	04/30/59	05/26/59	EA	N5531		WO		07/02/76; Boston, MA
1056	A	05/07/59	05/13/59	AA	N6114A	PF		Transafrik (S9-NAH)	
1057	C	07/01/59	07/19/59	NW	N121US		WO		03/17/60; Tell City, IN
1058	A	05/17/59	05/18/59	AA	N6115A		BU		1975; Wilmington, OH
1059	A	05/15/59	05/25/59	NA	N5002K	AF	WO		03/12/76; Lake Udrivik, AK
1060	A	05/13/59	06/02/59	EA	N5532	AF		Conair (C-FZCS)	
1061	A	05/19/59	06/15/59	TA	VH-TLA	AF	BU		03/76; Seletar, Singapore
1062	A	05/23/59	06/08/59	EA	N5533		WO		10/04/60; Boston, MA
1063	A	05/27/59	06/04/59	AA	N6116A				converted to tanker
1064	A	06/04/59	06/12/59	NA	N5003K	AF	WO	Air Spray (C-FQYB)	12/11/74; Deadhorse, AK
1065	A	06/09/59	06/17/59	AA	N6117A		BU		03/71; Tulsa, OK
1066	A	06/15/59	06/25/59	EA	N5534	AF	BU		Greenville, NC
1067	A	06/59	06/22/59	BN	N9703C		Preserved		Cmde. Espora, Argentina
1068	A	06/59	07/09/59	EA	N5535	AF	WO	Channel Express (G-CHNX)	
1069	A	06/59	07/14/59	TA	VH-TLB	AF	WO		02/02/80; San Salvador, El Salvador
1070	C	06/59	07/10/59	WA	N7136C	PF		Argentine Navy (6-P-103)	
1071	C	07/21/59	07/27/59	EA	N5536		BU		11/82; Bahia Blanca, Argentina
1072	A	07/16/59	07/25/59	AA	N6118A	AF		Argentine Navy (6-P-104)	
1073	A	07/28/59	08/01/59	AA	N6119A			Trans Service Airlift (9Q-CRM)	
1074	A	07/24/59	07/29/59	WA	N7137C	AF	BU		05/83; Marana, AZ
1075	C	08/04/59	08/13/59	EA	N5537		CF	Channel Express (G-OFRT)	
1076	A	08/02/59	08/06/59	NA	N5004K	AF	WO		07/06/77; St. Louis, MO
1077	C	07/21/59	07/29/59	NW	N122US	CF		Aerocondor (HK-1845)	stored; Barranquilla, Colombia
1078	C	08/10/59	08/20/59	EA	N5538				stored; Asuncion, Paraguay
1079	A	08/12/59	08/17/59	NA	N5005K	AF		Lynden Air Cargo (N281F)	
1080	C	08/13/59	08/28/59	EA	N5539		WO		12/18/95; Kahengula, Angola
1081	C	08/13/59	08/17/59	AA	N6120A			Aerocondor (HK-1415)	stored; Barranquilla, Colombia
1082	C	08/04/59	08/11/59	NW	N123US	AF		Air Spray (C-FVFI)	converted to tanker
1083	A	08/18/59	08/22/59	AA	N6121A			Aerocondor (HK-774)	stored; Barranquilla, Colombia
1084	A	08/18/59	08/30/59	NA	N5006K	AF		Zantop (N282F)	stored; Detroit-Willow Run
1085	C	08/26/59	08/30/59	NW	N124US	CF	BU		fire pit trainer; Greenville, SC
1086	A	08/22/59	08/28/59	BN	N9704C		WO		12/24/71; Puerto Inca, Peru
1087	A	08/20/59	09/04/59	WA	N7138C	AF	WO		07/10/75; Bogota, Colombia
1088	C	08/01/59	09/17/59	EA	N5540	CF		Trans Union Leasing (N5540)	stored; Miami, FL
1089	A	08/29/59	09/04/59	NA	N5007K	AF	WO		04/30/75; Deadhorse, AK
1090	A	09/04/59	09/18/59	BN	N9705C		WO		09/29/59; Buffalo, TX
1091	C	10/22/59	11/06/59	PS	N171PS	CF		Channel Express (G-CEXS)	
1092	A	09/18/59	09/24/59	NA	N5008K	CF		Spirit of America (N666F)	stored
1093	A	09/01/59	09/23/59	AA	N6122A		BU		02/95; Kinshasa, Zaire

msn	model	First Flight	Del. Date	Original Operator	Registr	Cargo Conv.	Current Status	Current/Last Known Operator (Registration)	Notes
1094	A	09/11/59	09/26/59	WA	N7139C	PF	BU		03/93; Greenville, SC
1095	A	09/23/59	10/01/59	BN	N9706C		BU	LANSA (OB-R-945)	derelict; Lima, Peru
1096	A	09/29/59	10/05/59	NA	N5009K	CF	BU		10/90; Aruba
1097	A	10/02/59	10/10/59	NA	N5010K		BU		1974; Miami, FL
1098	C	10/06/59	10/14/59	EA	N5541		CF	Fred Olsens (LN-FOO)	stored; Coventry, UK
1099	A	10/13/59	10/17/59	BN	N9707C		WO		05/03/68; Dawson, TX
1100	A	10/06/59	10/22/59	AA	N6123A	AF	BU	Atlantic Airlines (G-LOFC)	
1101	C	10/15/59	10/22/59	NW	N125US	CF	BU		12/18; Miami, FL
1102	A	10/15/59	10/23/59	AA	N6124A	PF	BU	Argentine Navy (5-T-1)	
1103	C		12/10/61	FAA	N111		BU		1997; Davis Monthan AFB, AZ
1104	A	10/01/59	11/03/59	NA	N5011K	AF		Zantop (N284F)	stored; Detroit-Willow Run
1105	C	11/06/59	11/14/59	NW	N126US	CF	WO		06/30/77; offshore of Panama
1106	A	11/12/59	11/17/59	BN	N9708C		WO		08/09/70; Cuzco, Peru
1107	A	11/18/59	11/24/59	NA	N5012K	AF		Renown Aviation (N285F)	
1108	C	11/18/59	11/25/59	NW	N127US		BU		1974; Van Nuys, CA
1109	C	11/21/59	11/30/59	PS	N172PS	CF		Zantop (N340HA)	stored; Detroit-Willow Run
1110	C	12/03/59	12/09/59	PS	N173PS	CF		Lynden Air Cargo (N289F)	
1111	C	12/05/59	12/10/59	NW	N128US		WO		8/92; location unconfirmed
1112	C	11/25/59	12/15/59	NW	N129US	CF		Channel Express (N360Q)	stored; Bournemouth, UK
1113	C	12/19/59	12/30/59	NW	N130US			Legion Express (N188LE)	
1114	A	12/31/59	01/09/60	BN	N9709C		BU		Jakarta, Indonesia
1115	A	12/22/59	12/31/59	AA	N6125A		WO		08/23/73; Bogota, Colombia
1116	A	01/05/60	01/13/60	AA	N6126A	AF		Fred Olsens (LN-FOL)	stored; Coventry, UK
1117	A	01/08/60	01/21/60	AA	N6127A		WO		09/14/60; New York, NY
1118	A	01/12/60	01/21/60	WA	N7140C	PF	WO		11/05/74; Anchorage, AK
1119	A	01/13/60	01/27/60	AA	N6128A		WO		03/13/95; Kinshasa, Zaire
1120	A	01/22/60	02/03/60	AA	N6129A			Argentine Navy (6-P-106)	
1121	A	02/02/60	02/12/60	AA	N6130A		WO		01/21/85; Reno, NV
1122	A	02/09/60	02/17/60	AA	N6131A	PF		Argentine Navy (5-T-3)	stored; Buenos Aires, Argentina.
1123	A	02/12/60	02/19/60	AA	N6132A	AF		Argentine Navy (6-P-106)	
1124	A	02/19/60	02/24/60	AA	N6133A			Comm'l. Link Trade (HR-AMM)	
1125	A	02/22/60	02/25/60	AA	N6134A			TAM Bolivia (TAM-01)	stored; La Paz, Bolivia
1126	A	03/04/60	03/21/60	AA	N6135A		WO		01/21/94; Kinshasa, Zaire
1127	A	12/31/60	03/24/61	WA	N7141C	PF	WO		01/05/79; North Slope, AK
1128	A	01/01/61	05/17/61	WA	N7142C	PF		Fred Olsens (LN-FON)	stored; Coventry, UK
1129	A	03/30/60	05/24/61	WA	N7143C	PF		Atlantic Airlines (G-FIJV)	
1130	C	04/26/60	01/31/62	PS	N175PS			NCAR (N308D)	
1131	C	10/28/60	03/09/61	NW	N131US	CF		Atlantic Airlines (G-LOFB)	
1132	C	12/16/60	03/10/61	NW	N132US		WO		03/31/77; CFB Summerside, Canada

msn	model	First Flight	Del. Date	Original Operator	Registr	Cargo Conv.	Current Status	Current/Last Known Operator (Registration)	Notes
1133	C	06/22/60	01/31/62	SA	N182H		CF	Zantop (N290F)	stored; Detroit-Willow Run
1134	C	12/17/60	05/10/62	BN	N9710C	CF	WO		03/21/90; near Tegucigalpa, Honduras
1135	C	12/01/60	02/26/62	SA	N184H	CF	BU		11/96; Opa-locka, FL
1136	C	01/01/61	02/26/62	SA	N185H		WO		04/22/66; Ardmore, OK
1137	C	01/18/61	03/14/61	NW	N133US	PF		Filair (9Q-CUU)	
1138	C	01/31/61	03/29/61	NW	N134US	PF		Atlantic Airlines (G-FIJR)	
1139	C	03/30/61	04/07/61	NW	N135US	PF	WO		8/94; Angola
1140	A	01/24/61	02/03/61	WA	N9744C	PF		Reeve Aleutian	
1141	C	05/12/61	05/23/61	NW	N136US	PF	WO		10/30/74; near Rea Point, Canada
1142	C	06/02/61	06/22/61	NW	N137US		WO		09/16/61; Chicago, IL
1143	A	02/07/61	02/15/61	WA	N9745C	AF		Atlantic Airlines (G-LOFD)	
1144	C	06/06/61	06/23/61	NW	N138US	CF		Atlantic Airlines (EI-CET)	Being parted out; East Midlands, UK
1145	A	01/31/61	02/09/61	WA	N9746C	AF		Amerer Air (OE-ILA)	
1146	A	08/16/60	01/06/61	NA	N5013K	AF		Zantop (N286F)	stored; Detroit-Willow Run
1147	A	08/16/61	08/25/61	TA	VH-TLC	AF		Transapel (HK-3706X)	
1148	A	12/16/60	01/09/61	NA	N5014K	AF		Lynden Air Cargo (N287F)	
2001	C	06/06/59	09/21/59	KL	PH-LLA	CF	WO		03/19/72; Hill AFB, Ogden, UT
2002	C	09/17/59	10/30/59	QF	VH-ECA	CF	BU		05/98; Coventry, UK
2003	C	10/01/59	10/10/59	KL	PH-LLB	CF	BU		08/17/98; East Midlands, UK
2004	C	10/03/59	10/30/59	QF	VH-ECB		WO		09/04/89; Taura AFB, Ecuador
2005	C	10/14/59	10/15/89	TE	ZK-TEA	CF		Fred Olsens (LN-FOI)	stored; Coventry, UK
2006	C	10/24/59	11/19/59	KL	PH-LLC	CF		Hunting Cargo (EI-CHX)	stored; East Midlands, UK
2007	C	11/19/59	11/24/59	QF	VH-ECC			Reeve Aleutian (N1968R)	
2008	C	11/25/59	12/03/59	QF	VH-ECD	CF	WO		11/30/85; Medan, Indonesia
2009	C	12/05/59	12/16/59	KL	PH-LLD	CF	WO		01/29/85; Marietta, GA
2010	C	12/10/59	12/18/59	TE	ZK-TEB	PF		Reeve Aleutian (N178RV)	
2011	C	12/04/59	12/14/59	TE	ZK-TEC	CF	WO		03/27/65; Whenuapai Airport, N.Z.
2012	C	12/04/59	01/30/60	KL	PH-LLE	CF	WO		08/24/70; Hill AFB, Ogden, UT
2013	C	01/27/60	02/16/60	KL	PH-LLF	CF		Transcarga (N107DH)	stored; Tucson, AZ
2014	C	02/17/60	02/25/60	KL	PH-LLG	CF		Atlantic Airlines (G-FIJU)	
2015	C	03/26/60	04/16/60	KL	PH-LLH	CF	BU		08/18/98; East Midlands, UK
2016	C	04/06/60	04/29/60	KL	PH-LLI	CF	WO		11/18/79; Granger, UT
2017	C	04/29/60	05/14/60	KL	PH-LLK	CF	BU		1989; for spares
2018	C	11/19/60	12/01/60	KL	PH-LLL	CF	BU		11/96; Opa-locka, FL
2019	C	12/05/60	12/14/60	KL	PH-LLM	CF	WO		06/12/61; Cairo, Egypt
2020	C	12/12/60	01/14/61	GA	PK-GLA		BU		Jakarta, Indonesia
2021	C	12/60/60	01/24/61	GA	PK-GLB		WO		02/16/67; Manado, Indonesia
2022	C	01/11/61	01/15/61	GA	PK-GLC	CF		Transapel (HK-3716X)	

HP-579 (msn 1011), COPA's first Electra in its final color scheme, stripped of parts and ready for scrapping at Mojave, California. (Terry Waddington)

Msn 1074 was scrapped at Marana, Arizona, in 1983. (Jon Proctor)

Mojave is the end of the road for another Electra. (David G. Powers)

Appendix IV
BIBLIOGRAPHY

Allen, Richard S. *Revolution in the Sky*. New York, New York: Orion Books, 1988.

Cohen, Stan. *Flying Beats Work – The Story of Reeve Aleutian Airways*. Missoula, Montana: Pictorial Histories Publishing, 1988.

Davies, R.E.G. *Airlines of Latin America since 1919*. London: Putnam, 1984.
– *Airlines of the United States since 1914*. Washington, D.C.: Smithsonian, 1972.

Denhan, Terry. *World Directory of Airline Crashes*. Somerset, U.K.: PSL, 1996.

Eastwood, A.B. & Roach, J. *Turbo Prop Airliners Production List*. Ruslip, Middlesex, U.K.: The Aviation Hobby Shop, 1998.

Francillion, Rene J. *Lockheed Aircraft since 1913*. Annapolis, Maryland: Naval Institute, 1987.

Green, William & Swanborough, Gordon & Mowinski, John. *Modern Commercial Aircraft*. New York, New York: Portland House, 1987.

Hopkins, George E. *Flying the Line*. Washington, D.C.: The Airline Pilots Association, 1982.

Ingells, Douglas J. *L-1011 TriStar and the Lockheed Story*. Fallbrook, California: Aero Publishers, Inc. 1973.

Johnson, Clarence L. & Smith, Maggie. *Kelly – More Than My Share of it All*. Washington, D.C.: Smithsonian, 1985.

Loughead, Victor. *Vehicles of the Air*. Chicago, Illinois: Reilly and Britton Co., 1909

Milberry, Larry. *Air Transport In Canada*. Toronto, Ontario: CANAV books, 1997.

Nance, John J. *Splash of Colors*. New York, New York: Morrow and Co., 1984.

Rich, Ben R. & Janos, Leo. *Skunk Works*. Boston, Massachusetts: Little, Brown and Co., 1994.

Ruble, Kenneth, D. *Flight to the Top*. Kenneth D. Ruble, 1986.

Serling, Robert J. *Eagle – The Story of American Airlines*. New York: St. Martin's/Marek, 1985.
– *The Electra Story*. New York: Doubleday, 1963.
– *From the Captain to the Colonel*. New York: Dial Press, 1980.
– *The Only Way to Fly*. New York: Doubleday, 1976.

Scharschmidt, Oliver. *Cargo Airlines*. Osceola, WI: Motorbooks, 1997

Stringfellow, C.K. & Bowers, Peter M. *Lockheed Constellation*. Osceola, WI: Motorbooks, 1992.

Wegg, John. *General Dynamics Aircraft and their Predecessors*. Annapolis, MD: Naval Institute, 1990.

Too numerous to be listed by date, the following periodicals, guidebooks and fleet lists also provided an invaluable source of information: *Air Enthusiast, Air International, Air Transport News, Airliners, Aviation-Letter, Aviation Week and Space Technology, Flying, jp airline-fleets international, Logbook, Propliner, Single Digit Computing – Lockheed Jet Production List, World Airline Fleets News.*

Finally, the wealth of knowledge gleaned from Lockheed Martin in-house publications cannot be overemphasized.

Terry Waddington Collection